Stephen Plant is senior tutor and director of studies at Wesley House, Cambridge. He teaches theology and ethics in the Cambridge Theological Federation and is an affiliated lecturer in the University of Cambridge Faculty of Divinity. He is a regular contributor to *The Times* newspaper and is the author or editor of several books, including *Bonhoeffer* (Continuum, 2004).

SIMONE WEIL
A Brief Introduction

Stephen Plant

ORBIS BOOKS
Maryknoll, New York 10545

Founded in 1970, Orbis Books endeavors to publish works that enlighten the mind, nourish the spirit, and challenge the conscience. The publishing arm of the Maryknoll Fathers and Brothers, Orbis seeks to explore the global dimensions of the Christian faith and mission, to invite dialogue with diverse cultures and religious traditions, and to serve the cause of reconciliation and peace. The books published reflect the views of their authors and do not represent the official position of the Maryknoll Society. To learn more about Maryknoll and Orbis Books, please visit our website at www.maryknoll.org.

First published in Great Britain in 1996 as *Simone Weil* by Fount Paperbacks, an imprint of HarperCollins Publishers.

This revised and expanded edition first published in Great Britain in 2007 by Society for Promoting Christian Knowledge, 36 Causton Street, London SW1P 4ST.

First published in the United States of America in 2008 by Orbis Books, P.O. Box 308, Maryknoll, NY 10545-0308.

The publisher and author acknowledge with thanks permission to reproduce extracts from:
Gravity and Grace by Simone Weil, translated by Arthur Wills, copyright 1952, renewal © 1980 by G. P. Putnam's Sons. Original French copyright 1947 by Librairie Plon. Used by permission of G. P. Putnam's Sons, a division of Penguin Group (USA) Inc.
Waiting for God by Simone Weil, translated by Emma Craufurd, copyright 1951, renewed © 1979 by G. P. Putnam's Sons. Used by permission of G. P. Putnam's Sons, a division of Penguin Group (USA) Inc.

Unless otherwise indicated, Scripture quotations are from the New Revised Standard Version of the Bible, copyright © 1989 by the Division of Christian Education of the National Council of the Churches of Christ in the USA. Used by permission. All rights reserved.

Typeset by Graphicraft Ltd, Hong Kong.
Printed in Great Britain by Ashford Colour Press.
Produced on paper from sustainable forests.

Library of Congress Cataloging-in-Publication Data

Plant, Stephen.
Simone Weil: a brief introduction / Stephen Plant.—Rev. and expanded ed., 2nd ed.
p. cm.
Includes bibliographical references (p.   ) and index.
ISBN-13: 978–1–57075–753–2
1. Weil, Simone, 1909–1943.   2. Weil, Simone, 1909–1943—Religion.   3. Philosophers—France—Biography.   I. Title.
B2430.W474P57 2008
230.092—dc22

2007029573

Contents

Preface to the second edition

This book was commissioned for a British series that aims to introduce thinkers who have made a significant contribution to Christian thought to as wide an audience as possible in as intelligible a way as possible. It is an aim Simone Weil would have approved of. Though herself highly educated and uniquely intellectually gifted, Weil believed that the questions addressed by politics and philosophy, by literature and theology were too important to be confined to those with a high level of formal academic training. It was fundamental to her that the most profound insights in the history of human thought can and should be made accessible to all. She was surely right.

She was also right to assert that ultimately, the thing that matters, the thing we are seeking in literature, philosophy and theology, is not what it tells us about the author but what it tells us about truth. In one of her books, Weil asked a question that should daunt anyone preparing to explore her thought, and even more, anyone setting out to write about it:

> Are there many books or articles which leave us with the impression that the author, first before ever beginning to write, and then again before handing the manuscript to the printer, asked himself with any real concern: 'Am I in line with truth?' Are there many readers who, before opening a book, ask themselves with any real concern: 'Am I going to find truth in here?' (NR 257)

This book first appeared in 1996.* Preparing a new edition of a text written more than a decade ago has proved to be a

---

* *Simone Weil*, London, Fount, 1996; US edition: Liguori, Mo., Triumph Books, 1996; Spanish translation: *Simone Weil: Pensadores Cristianos*, Barcelona, Herder, 1997.

strange experience in which I have found myself in conversation not only with Simone Weil, but with a younger 'me'. The task of writing a second edition certainly gives rise to a number of vexing issues, chief of which is the extent to which one revises the text in the light of one's present preoccupations and perspectives. Since I first worked on Weil I have become clearer about my own views of her writings. I have read more of the secondary literature – some of it rich in raising issues and offering insights to which I was oblivious in 1996 – that engages with her life and thought. I have become more aware of the importance of her distinctive reading of the writings of Plato, grown more appreciative of the illumination achieved in her essays on science, and have come to view her thinking less in episodes and more as an integrated series. I am much more disturbed by her antipathy to Jews, to Judaism and to the Hebrew Scriptures and more conscious of the significance of this in making sense of her writings. In short, I have grown more sympathetic towards Simone Weil as a person, but I have become more alert – as the result of several years spent teaching Christian doctrine – to a number of significant theological questions raised by her writings.

I have made significant revisions and additions throughout, but the main structural change has been the replacement of the brief conclusion in the first edition with a new and longer Chapter 5, in which I begin to comment upon Simone Weil's life and thought from the perspective of Christian theology. I conclude with a guide to further reading in English.

Throughout this book, where I have cited Simone Weil I have used the English translation to be found in the most recent available edition. These translations were, however, written before translators became sensitized to gender-exclusive language. In what follows, therefore, I have allowed quotations from Weil to stand as they appear in the available translations – even where (as in 'there is something sacred in every man') it jars with those, like me, who otherwise favour using gender-inclusive language where possible.

The first edition of *Simone Weil* was part of a series edited by Peter Vardy. I remain very grateful to him, in inviting me to contribute, for taking a punt on a rookie in philosophical theology. The idea for the present edition came from Rebecca Mulhearn of SPCK, who has provided just the right balance of efficiency and encouragement in the months in which I have worked on it. I am also grateful to several groups of students in Cambridge who have participated in my classes on political theology and whose questions and comments have helped to sharpen my thinking about 'Sainte Simone'.

The first edition of *Simone Weil* appeared a few weeks before my marriage to Kirsty Smith, to whom it was dedicated. She gave me a scare at our wedding breakfast when in her speech she announced that she had wearied of competing for my attention with 'another woman', before conjuring *Simone Weil* from her sleeve. I am glad now to renew the book's dedication and to add my continuing gratitude for the adventure of her friendship.

Stephen Plant

Abbreviations

FLN	*First and Last Notebooks*
FW	*Formative Writings 1929–1941*
GG	*Gravity and Grace*
GWG	*Gateway to God*
IC	*Intimations of Christianity among the Ancient Greeks*
LP	*Lectures in Philosophy*
N	*The Notebooks of Simone Weil, volumes 1 and 2*
NR	*The Need for Roots*
OL	*Oppression and Liberty*
SE	*Selected Essays*
SL	*Seventy Letters*
SNLG	*On Science, Necessity, and the Love of God*
WG	*Waiting on God*

Details of editions cited are given in the guide to further reading in English that follows Chapter 5.

Date chart

Life of Simone Weil	General events
1909 3 February, Simone Weil born in Paris	
	1914 Outbreak of First World War
	1917 Russian Revolution
	1918 End of First World War
1925 Enters Lycée Henri IV	
1928 Enters École Normale Supérieure	
	1929 Wall Street Crash
1930 Weil's headaches begin	
1931 Starts teaching	
1932 Makes six-week visit to Berlin	
	1933 Hitler appointed Reich Chancellor
1934 Writes *Oppression and Liberty* Begins working in a factory	
1935 Holiday in Spain and Portugal	1935 Italy invades Abyssinia
1936 Weil enrols in the Anarchist Militia	1936 Spanish Civil War begins
1938 Visit to Solesmes – first mystical experiences	

Life of Simone Weil	*General events*
	1939 Hitler invades Poland – Second World War begins
1940 Weil family travel to Marseilles	1940 June – France surrenders
1941 Begins notebooks from which *Gravity and Grace* is later extracted	1941 The USA enters the war
1941 June – meets Fr Perrin Works for Gustave Thibon Writes most of the essays of *Intimations of Christianity among the Ancient Greeks*	
1942 Leaves France; travels to the USA via Casablanca Arrives in London in December	
1943 Writes *The Need for Roots* 15 April, enters Middlesex Hospital 24 August, Weil dies in Ashford, Kent	
	1945 Allied victory in Europe

Introduction
The importance of Simone Weil

Introducing someone's writing is always a dubious enterprise when their own words can speak for themselves. It is, in the words of a Buddhist proverb about teachers of religion, like trying to sell water beside a river. Nevertheless, when a writer's thought is as complex and challenging as Simone Weil's, there may be a role for the kind of introduction found in this book. Time is precious, and introductions help one decide whether a writer is worth making an effort to understand. An introduction may even assist the understanding of some ideas better than if one wrestled with them alone. It is my hope that this book will lead its readers into the writings of Simone Weil herself.

The inclusion of Weil in this series introducing thinkers significant for Christian thought and theology is remarkable for at least two reasons. First, Weil's impact is the more notable because she is a woman. A photograph, taken in 1926 of students at the Lycée Henri IV, shows rows of sharp and eager men ready to take on the world; a mere handful of women are scattered among them, one of whom is Simone Weil. In inter-war Europe, philosophy and politics, Weil's chosen fields, were, like so much else, worlds in which women were still unusual and in which, therefore, they had to work unusually hard to make their way. Even more was this the case in the spheres of the Church and of Christian thought, because the typical route to a rounded theological education through training for ordination was closed to most women. The Church has historically not found it easy to recognize the distinctive contribution that women bring to its life and thought. Thankfully, the late twentieth century witnessed growing recognition of the distinctive contribution of women to Church life and to Christian theology, but Weil remains something of an anomaly in being a woman who has played an important role in twentieth-century philosophical theology. Sensitive to the condition of women in history through her literary studies and aware from personal experience of the distinctive challenges faced by women in both politics and in the workplace, Weil has sometimes been called an icon of feminism. Certainly, her inclusion as a leading Christian thinker signals the crucial importance of women to Christian theology.

A second remarkable feature of Weil's inclusion in this series is that the question of whether she may be described as a *Christian* thinker is itself one of the most contested questions to arise from reflection upon her life and thought. She loved Jesus Christ and found in his cross the proof of Christianity. She yearned for the bread and wine of the Eucharist. Yet Weil resisted baptism, saw in the institutional Church the 'devil disguised', and rejected most of its Scriptures. Moreover, she engaged sympathetically with subjects on which the Church had remained largely silent – such as parallels between the Gospels and Greek mythology – or in some cases to which it had voiced deep antipathy – such as the writings of Karl Marx. Is it possible that Simone Weil's thinking, which traversed sacred and profane and bridged gaps between theology and other forms of human reasoning, can aid Christian thinking and action today? Is Weil's writing a resource for Christian theology? Is she a saint or a heretic? Such questions matter, but the only way to evaluate them is to pay to her writings the kind of attention to which she herself aspired in reading others' writings.

So why read Simone Weil? One reason might be the respect others have for her thought and writings. If such commendations are needed then there is no shortage of people ready to supply them. Simone de Beauvoir, the seminal feminist writer, felt daunted by Weil's reputed intelligence and envied

her 'heart that could beat right across the world'. The novelist André Gide called her 'the best spiritual writer of this
century', while the poet T. S. Eliot said she had a genius akin
to the saints. Her spiritual writings deeply impressed Pope
John XXIII, and Pope Paul VI's spiritual autobiography reports
that she was one of the three most important influences on
his intellectual development. Albert Camus regarded her as
the most penetrating and prophetic social and political thinker
since Marx, and stopped off to meditate in her room before
travelling to pick up his Nobel Prize for Literature. Leon
Trotsky stayed in her family home in Paris in 1933, where
they quarrelled. In exasperation with what he took to be her
revolutionary melancholia he asked if she belonged to the
Salvation Army, but he was clearly impressed by her readiness
to hold her own. And in her major philosophical work Iris
Murdoch, philosopher and novelist, regularly cites Weil as a
philosophical and literary authority. Of course, she also had
her detractors: that acute judge of character Charles de Gaulle
exclaimed: 'The woman was mad!'

The opinions of others are important, and the fact that so
many men and women of vastly differing views have found
Weil worth grappling with should be taken seriously.
Ultimately, however, the opinions expressed by others are not
good enough reasons to read Weil. As a teacher she herself
encouraged her pupils always to make up their own minds.

If it is not sufficient to take someone else's word that she
is worth reading, perhaps we should read Weil simply because
of her breadth of knowledge. She trained primarily in philosophy but also studied history and wrote essays on an unusually broad range of subjects. She wrote on classical Greek
philosophy, on classical Rome, on medieval France and on
Renaissance Florence. She wrote on geometry and on science.
She wrote on political subjects: on Marxist theory, on the
rise of Nazism and on colonialism. She developed theories on
the economy and on how working in a factory should be

restructured to make it more effective and more fruitful. As well as philosophical and historical approaches, she used the disciplines of sociology and anthropology to aid reflection on her subjects. And, of course, she wrote about philosophical theology as well, where her lack of formal theological training gave her a freshness of approach to many themes done to death by professional theologians. Yet even breadth of knowledge need not be a good thing if accompanied by shallowness. The expansiveness of Weil's learning and the extraordinary range of subjects about which she wrote are worthwhile only if what she has to say is worth attention.

Perhaps she should be read because of her intelligence. When in 1927 the results in the BA in Philosophy were declared at the Sorbonne in Paris, Weil was top of the lists, with de Beauvoir second. In 1931, out of 107 candidates at the renowned École Normale Supérieure, only 11 passed and Weil came seventh. She grew up speaking French and German at home; she learned Spanish and English; she was a gifted translator of classical Greek and could read Sanskrit and Tibetan.

But not even her intelligence is good enough reason to devote attention to her thought. She once wrote that a person who celebrates his own intelligence is like a man condemned to imprisonment who shows off the size of his cell. Cleverness is not to be confused with wisdom; intelligence has value only to the extent that it is used in pursuit of the truth. In one of her notebooks Weil jotted down the only thing intelligence can really achieve: 'We know by means of our intelligence that what the intelligence does not comprehend is more real than what it does comprehend' (GG 128).

Neither the recommendation of others, nor the breadth of her learning, nor the sharpness of her intelligence provides sufficient reason to read Simone Weil. It is not even worth reading Simone Weil merely to write an essay or to pass an exam. The only thing that mattered to Weil in her many writings, and the only really good reason for reading this book and books by her, is that what she thinks might be 'true'. In one of her last letters she wrote:

> I have a sort of growing inner certainty that there is within me a deposit of pure gold which must be handed on. Only I become more and more convinced, by experience, and by observing my contemporaries, that there is no one to receive it . . . This does not distress me at all. The mine of gold is inexhaustible. (SL 196ff.)

The purpose of this introduction is to mine the vein of gold her thought contains. It is not Simone Weil who will be the object of this study, but those things about which she thought so deeply and wrote so well.

Of course, fitting the breadth and profundity of Weil's thought into this slim volume is an impossible task. It is like getting a reluctant genie into his bottle. In Chapter 1, the main events in Weil's short life will be sketched out. This will provide a context in which to consider her writings. More than most thinkers, Weil's life and thought were intertwined, and so although the main aim of the book is to explore her thought, her brief biography is essential to an understanding of what she wrote. Chapters 2, 3 and 4 present the key subjects that are of value in Weil's intellectual legacy. Chapter 5 begins to open Weil's thought to some theological questions, and is followed by suggestions for further reading.

1

Simone Weil's life

A barren fig tree?

Simone Weil was haunted by self-doubt but also by a powerful awareness of the love of God. In 1942, the year before her death, Weil summed up her life in a letter to a friend. Comparing herself with the fig tree Jesus cursed while entering Jerusalem because it did not bear any fruit, she wrote:

> I never read the story of the barren fig tree without trembling. I think that it is a portrait of me. In it also, nature was powerless, and yet it was not excused. Christ cursed it . . .
>
> It is not that I actually do fear [God's anger]. By a strange twist, the thought of God's anger only arouses love in me. It is the thought of the possible favour of God and his mercy that makes me tremble with a sort of fear.
>
> On the other hand the sense of being like a barren fig tree for Christ tears my heart. (WG 64)

Weil's characterization of her life as barren and fruitless shows her profound lack of self-confidence. Yet taking the facts of her life at face value, her self-assessment is pitifully accurate. During her life most of her writings were almost unknown, even to her closest friends. Those of her essays that were published reached small audiences, and her larger essays became known only after her death. The trade union movement to which she devoted so much of the energy of her early life was riven with disagreement and was never diverted by her campaigning towards the goals she hoped for it. As a factory labourer seeking solidarity with the working classes, she was so exhausted that she was incapable of a full engagement with either her co-workers or with the experience. The injury that forced her exit from the Spanish Civil War was caused not by a fascist bullet or shell, but was the accidental result of her own clumsiness. In the Second World War she yearned for dangerous front-line action, but ended up in a London desk job. She lived to see neither the fall of the 'Great Beast' of Nazism, nor the regeneration of France. She longed for love, and lived the life of an outsider.

Simone Weil was born in Paris in 1909. Her only brother, André, was born three years earlier. Weil's father was a doctor in general practice. Her mother, though not trained in medicine because her father would not give his permission, poured her considerable intellectual energies into supporting her husband's career and in nurturing their precociously gifted children. She was by all accounts, including Simone's own, the more dominant of her parents, and some psychoanalytically inclined commentators have traced Simone's supposed difficulties with forming close relationships to a cloyingly possessive quality in Mme Weil's relationship with her daughter. Already, at 16 months, Simone found eating a problem, possibly the first indication of a life-long difficulty with food that some have subsequently (and speculatively) diagnosed as anorexia nervosa. A childhood stint in hospital didn't help, and she disliked hospitals thereafter. Whatever may have been the origin of her attitude to food, it is certainly the case that she persistently neglected her bodily need for a healthy diet. And Mme Weil could be obsessive about hygiene, which also rubbed off on Simone.

Weil's parents were Jewish, but neither practised their religion. Both Dr Weil's atheism (a reaction against the zealous piety of his mother), and the family's desire in all things to identify with middle-class French culture and patriotism, were important factors in Simone's upbringing. Alfred Dreyfus, a Jewish officer falsely imprisoned in 1893 for treason, was released just three years before Simone was born; what the Dreyfus affair made plain was that anti-Semitism was a living issue in early twentieth-century France. Quite apart from any 'philosophical' reasons the empirically inclined Dr Weil may have had for breaking off ties with Jewish communities in France, there were good reasons for assimilating. But for Jews who chose to break such ties there were practical as well as psychological consequences that affected not only the first, but following generations, who sometimes felt equally alien in the community they had been estranged from and in the (anti-Semitic) community they aspired to be part of. In an uncompromising letter written in 1940, Simone Weil explained her attitude towards her Jewish inheritance to an official in Vichy France tasked with registering Jews as the state had been 'encouraged' to do by the Nazis. If by 'Jew' one means a follower of a particular religion, Weil wrote, then 'I have never entered a synagogue and I have never witnessed a Jewish religious ceremony'. If one means by 'Jew' a member of a particular race, she continued, then 'I have no reason to suppose that I have any sort of tie, either through my father or my mother, with the people who lived in Palestine two thousand years ago'.

During the First World War, Weil's father served as an army doctor: as he moved from garrison to garrison the family moved with him from town to town. André and Simone were particularly close, but the proximity came at a cost. André had a brilliant mind: at 12 he was solving mathematical problems at a doctoral level, and to relax, reading Plato and Homer in Greek. Simone compared herself unfavourably with him, a comparison others unfortunately colluded in. Later she wrote that:

> The exceptional gifts of my brother, who had a childhood and youth comparable to those of Pascal [the French mathematician and philosopher], brought my own inferiority home to me. (WG 30)

She describes how this led her to fall into a bottomless adolescent despair, since she 'preferred to die rather than live without the truth' from which, aged 14, she had convinced herself her 'mediocrity' would exclude her. But after some months she

> ... suddenly had the everlasting conviction that no matter what human being, even though practically devoid of natural faculties, can penetrate to the kingdom reserved for geniuses, if only he longs for truth and perpetually concentrates all his attention upon its attainment.
>
> (WG 30–31)

This insight, imprinted on her adolescent mind, remained with her vividly throughout her life.

By the time Weil arrived in her mid-teens, she had already decided to choose philosophy rather than mathematics as her future academic speciality. At 16 she enrolled at the prestigious Lycée Henri IV, where she studied French, English, history and philosophy. Her physical appearance at this age changed little during the rest of her life. One of her fellow students, her friend and later biographer Simone Pétrement, described Weil's distinctive appearance:

> [She had a] small, thin face, which seemed to be devoured by her hair and glasses. A fine-boned delicate nose, dark eyes that looked out boldly, a neck that strained forward and gave the impression of a burning, almost indiscreet curiosity; but her full mouth gave one a feeling of sweetness and good nature. Looking at them carefully her features do not lack charm and even beauty; it was a face at once insolent and tender, bold in asking questions but with a timid smile that seemed to mock itself ... Her charm remained hidden from most people, who saw in Simone only a totally intellectual being. Her body was thin, her gestures lively but also clumsy. She wore clothes with a masculine cut, always the same outfit

(a kind of suit with a very wide skirt and a long, narrow jacket), and always flat-heeled shoes.

(Simone Pétrement, *Simone Weil: A Life*, p. 26)

It is said that one of few women to study with Plato at his Academy, Axiothea, dressed as a man: if Weil knew of her, Axiothea might have made a good role-model.

Weil's philosophy teacher at the Lycée was the celebrated Emile Chartier, better known as 'Alain'. From him Weil learned how to express her ideas clearly and succinctly. He also taught her to respect the Greek philosopher Plato (427–347 BC), and reinforced her childhood love of geometry. At the end of her two years at the school she won the philosophy prize. Alain's final comment on his star pupil was characteristically perceptive. He noted that she was an

... excellent student; unusual strength of mind, broad culture. She will succeed brilliantly if she does not go down obscure paths. In any event she will certainly be noticed.

(Pétrement, p. 542)

In 1927, although she was placed first in examinations for the philosophy degree at the Sorbonne, she failed the broader and highly competitive entrance exams for the École Normale Supérieure, and was forced to study more widely before passing them a year later. Affiliated to the Sorbonne, the École Normale was one of the most respected academic institutions in France, giving its graduates access to teaching posts in France's best schools and entitling them to a higher salary. Weil studied there from 1928 to 1931, and entered fully into student life. She even joined a rugby team. In 1930, following an attack of viral sinusitis, Weil began experiencing migraine headaches. These were to afflict her with regular and excruciating ferocity for the rest of her life – a fact that should be borne in mind when examining the theme of affliction in Chapter 3. In July 1931, Weil qualified as a teacher and presented an extended dissertation on 'Science and Perception' in the work of the French philosopher René Descartes (1596–1650).

To recount Weil's student days in terms of her academic studies alone, however, is to tell only half the story. The years in Paris from 1925 to 1931 were also for Weil years in which she was deeply engaged in political reflection and action. These were eventful times as the political parties and organizations of the Left battled with one another. Weil was painfully aware of the debilitating effects of the splits in trade unions and political parties representing the interests of working people, and she toiled with little success for unity. In the USA, the Wall Street Crash shattered the illusion of worldwide economic prosperity. The repercussions were felt in France, where working people faced high unemployment and worsening working conditions. In 1927, Weil had worked long hours on a farm in Normandy bringing in the harvest. When she returned to Paris she began a Social Education Group with friends, giving free lessons in philosophy to factory and railway workers.

In this rapidly changing social environment, and with a personal conviction informed by her conversations with rural and industrial workers, Weil became ever more involved with politics. When a petition was drawn up campaigning against the compulsory military instruction given to male students at the École, she was vigorous in gathering signatures to make the training voluntary. She pestered one of her lecturers, M. Bouglé, for a donation to a fund for the unemployed. When the time came for the authorities to place her in a school, she asked to be placed in an industrial centre. Instead, with malicious intent, they posted her to Le Puy, a relatively quiet non-industrial town in south-eastern France. Bouglé, who had a hand in the decision, is reputed to have said: 'We shall send the Red Virgin as far away as possible so that we shall never hear of her again.'

From 1931 to 1934 Simone Weil taught philosophy in a series of schools. Her students liked her and in return she took a genuine interest in them. In a letter to a former student Weil asked if there was 'still the same good spirit of comradeship' among a class that she had taught. Her teaching methods, however, were somewhat unorthodox: she was less interested in her pupils passing exams than in inspiring them with her love of philosophy. From notes taken by her pupils it seems that what she actually taught was a brief history of Western thought. She explored basic philosophical questions like 'How do we perceive the world?' and 'How does language affect the way we come to grips with the world?' She also taught the basics of ethics, sociology and political science (these lectures are published as *Lectures in Philosophy*). To those who struggled with what they learned, she taught extra classes free of charge.

If her unconventional teaching practices prejudiced the school authorities against her, then her activities outside school made things even worse. From the point of view of her employers, Weil's life was inappropriate for a professional person. She disdained spending money on clothes or luxuries, buying books instead, and giving the rest of her salary to workers' strike funds. She refused to have the heating on in her room because, she believed, the unemployed had to live in the cold, and therefore she should too. In her support for the poor and unemployed of Le Puy she was untiring. She was also prominent in political demonstrations of various kinds and her name appeared in the local papers as a result. Once, Weil led a delegation to the local Mayor to ask for a rise in unemployment benefit. This kind of behaviour in a schoolteacher employed by the state was (not unreasonably) frowned upon by her employers. In consequence, she was moved three times in as many years, passed like a bad penny from Le Puy to Auxerre (1932), and from Auxerre to Roanne (1933). She taught her classes diligently, though without success if measured by examination results. Beyond the school gates she continued to meet local workers, to teach them in her spare time and to campaign for better conditions for workers and the unemployed.

Somehow, Weil also found time and energy to think and to write. In 1932 she spent six weeks in Germany observing the conflict between communists and Nazis at first hand; she wrote several essays reflecting on experiences and evaluating the rise and the political significance of Nazism. Her socialist friends were optimistic that a working-class revolution in Germany was imminent. Weil, however, believed that in spite of the heroism of individuals, the working classes were too disunited to achieve anything. She saw immediately that the Nazis were bad, but she also noted striking resemblances between National Socialism and communism. When published, these essays estranged her from many of her former friends. A number of the most important of Weil's political essays are collected in *Oppression and Liberty*.

By 1934 Weil had become convinced that the reason socialist leaders were so out of touch with working people was that none of them knew what it was like to work in a factory. She therefore obtained permission from the Ministry of Education to take a one-year 'sabbatical' for 'personal studies'. She was granted unpaid leave and, after a break to finish working on the key essays in *Oppression and Liberty*, on 4 December she began work as a factory hand in the Alsthom factory in Paris.

She worked at Alsthom for four months, after which she needed a period of convalescence in Switzerland to recover. In April 1935 she was back at work, this time at the Carnaud factory. In June she was working at the Renault plant. The journal Weil kept throughout her 'sabbatical', though dispassionately descriptive, records a painfully difficult year for her. It was, nevertheless, a year that led her in several new and fruitful directions. She had learned a great deal about living with affliction, and her high regard for manual labour remained undiminished. But the year had also, in her own words, left her 'in pieces, soul and body'.

During her summer holidays, Weil travelled in Spain and Portugal with her parents. In Portugal, on a solitary day's outing, she entered a small fishing village on the evening of a religious festival. The candle-light procession, and the hymns of 'heart-rending sadness' reached deep into her exhausted soul. Later, she wrote:

> ... the conviction was suddenly borne in upon me that Christianity is pre-eminently the religion of slaves, that slaves cannot help belonging to it, and I among others.
>
> (WG 34)

In October 1936, now aged 27, she was back teaching philosophy, this time at Bourges. She entered into a long correspondence with Monsieur Bernard, a factory manager, making various suggestions to him on how to run his factory. She also wrote a series of articles for his factory magazine introducing some of the classics of ancient Greek poetry and drama, for example on Homer's *Iliad*, and on Sophocles' *Antigone*. This was in keeping with the desire she had as a student to educate the working classes. It was also because she believed that the tragic themes of the classic dramas were more readily understood by people rooted in the ordinary world than by stuffy academic scholars. She also corresponded with Bernard in June 1936 when 'sit-in' strikes broke out across France. Unsurprisingly, Bernard did not share Weil's joy at seeing workers in control of whole factories.

In August of the same year, Weil's hunger for a cause led her to Spain, where civil war had erupted between fascists and a loose coalition of communists, socialists and anti-fascist 'loyalists'. Weil had always been a pacifist. In this instance, however, because she hoped so fervently for the victory of the anti-fascists, she believed she was already morally implicated in the conflict, and that she was therefore obliged to set aside her personal antipathy to violence. It was not her way to stay on the sidelines: she travelled to Barcelona and attempted to join a workers' militia. She latched on to a small international group, in which she had some acquaintances. After some days with this group she wanted to join a detachment moving to intercept a column of Franco's men, but to her chagrin her colleagues, who had noticed her extreme clumsiness with her rifle, refused to take her. She took part subsequently in a couple of relatively uneventful reconnaissance expeditions, and was bombed more than once. Her journal records her pride that she was only once scared during this period, and then it seems it was on behalf of some of her colleagues. On 20 August 1936, the short-sighted Weil fell into a pot of boiling cooking fat, set into the ground to screen the flames. The wound was quite serious and after a day or two she was back in Barcelona, her war prematurely ended. There her anxious parents found her and brought her back to France. To begin with, Weil had intended to return to Spain, but the 'smell of blood and terror' associated with civil war disillusioned her greatly. While in Spain, Weil had almost witnessed the execution of a priest by her own militia unit and had considered intervening on his behalf. On another occasion a 15-year-old youth was captured by the militia in which Weil had served. Given a day to consider changing sides, he declined and was promptly executed. Weil felt morally implicated in such instances of brutality by her own side, which lay heavily on her conscience.

After convalescing in Italy and Switzerland, Weil returned briefly to teaching, though with frequent periods of sick leave. In 1937 and 1938, Weil's life took a dramatic turn. Though she had considered God as a topic for philosophy, she had, at least in her writings, paid little attention to Christianity. Increasingly, Weil's difficult experiences as a factory worker and in Spain led her to reflect upon life's meaning and purpose, a line of enquiry that led ultimately to God. This left her open to several profound spiritual encounters. During a visit to Assisi in 1937, as Weil herself later recounted, something stronger than her own will compelled her for the first time to go down on her knees in prayer. A year later she spent Holy Week and Easter at the Benedictine monastery of Solesmes:

10

I was suffering from splitting headaches; each sound hurt me like a blow; by an extreme effort of concentration I was able to rise above this wretched flesh, to leave it to suffer by itself, heaped up in a corner, and to find a pure and perfect joy in the unimaginable beauty of the chanting and the words. This experience enabled me by analogy to get a better understanding of the possibility of loving divine love in the midst of affliction. It goes without saying that in the course of these services the thought of the Passion of Christ entered into my being once and for all.

(WG 34)

At Solesmes a young English Catholic led her to reflect upon the religious power of the sacraments. He introduced her to a poem by George Herbert, a seventeenth-century English poet, on the love of God.

Love bade me welcome: yet my soul drew back,
    Guiltie of dust and sinne.
But quick-ey'd Love, observing me grow slack
    From my first entrance in,
Drew nearer to me, sweetly questioning,
    If I lack'd any thing.

A guest, I answer'd, worthy to be here:
    Love said, You shall be he.
I the unkinde, ungratefull? Ah my deare,
    I cannot look on thee.
Love took my hand, and smiling did reply,
    Who made the eyes but I?

Truth Lord, but I have marr'd them: let my shame
    Go where it doth deserve.
And know you not, sayes Love, who bore the blame?
    My deare, then I will serve.
You must sit down, sayes Love, and taste my meat:
    So I did sit and eat.

She learned it by heart and would recite it to herself when the pain of her headaches was at its worst: 'It was during one of these recitations that, as I told you, Christ himself came down and took possession of me' (WG 35). A subject she had seen previously in terms of theoretical philosophy she now recast: 'in my arguments about the insolubility of the problem of God I had never foreseen the possibility . . . of a real contact, person to person, here below, between a human being and God' (WG 35). These experiences effected a redirection of her thought towards religious and theological themes.

In 1939, the world's drift towards war preoccupied Weil increasingly. She continued to write on classical Greek literature. On the eve of war she wrote about Homer's *Iliad*, but now drew out of this poem more of the cold brutality of violence and the ways in which the human spirit can resist it. When, in March, German troops entered Prague, she finally renounced pacifism. She drew parallels between Nazi Germany and ancient Rome at the height of its powers. Hitler, she argued, was the only leader in two thousand years who had learned to copy the Romans. Not only did the Romans believe themselves to be a superior race, they were also completely ruthless in their domination of other cities and cultures. Her antipathy towards the Nazis proved well founded when in September the Germans invaded Poland and world war broke out.

In 1940, Weil began to read Hindu Scriptures, particularly the *Bhagavad Gita*. For Weil, this classic text did not contradict but complemented Christianity. The way in which Weil arrived at this conclusion is explored in the next chapter.

With the outbreak of war Weil struggled to find the best way to react. Characteristically, she sought out a means to serve that would involve sharing the worst kinds of personal risk. She conceived a plan for front-line nurses, a plan she continued to advocate energetically and sometimes obsessively throughout the remainder of her life. Her idea was to form a mobile unit of female nurses available to give first-aid at the most dangerous parts of the front line of battle. She believed that it would have a moral effect on enemy and friend alike:

> The mere persistence of a few humane services in the very centre of the battle, the climax of inhumanity, would be a signal defiance of the inhumanity which the enemy has chosen for himself and which he compels us also to practise. (SL 144–5)

Though from time to time she managed to exploit her contacts with former student colleagues – many now in positions of responsibility – the plan never came to much; possibly Weil had failed to realize fully the extent to which war had changed since the trench warfare of the First World War. Innocent civilians were *already* caught in the crossfire, and that, moreover, with little morally moderating effect on the behaviour of forces committed to victory at any cost. Weil's plan is interesting chiefly because of what it tells us about her own convictions on how to respond to evil and to affliction.

In June 1940, France surrendered. Northern France, including Paris where the Weil family lived, was occupied by the Germans. Southern France, however, remained nominally independent, but with a government based in Vichy that was sympathetic to the Nazis. Whether or not the Weils considered themselves Jewish, they knew the Germans did. Thus, on the day the Germans were marching along one road into Paris, Dr Weil was inveigling himself, his wife and daughter onto the crowded last train out of the city, a journey that eventually brought them to the temporary safety of Vichy France.

The Weil family arrived in Marseilles in September 1940. Marseilles was the chief seaport of France, with a thriving cosmopolitan life. As she discovered more about the region in which Marseilles was situated, however, it was its history that captivated Weil. Between the eleventh and thirteenth centuries the region had been politically and culturally distinct from northern France. It was defined by a distinct language that gave the region its name, the Languedoc. The region had also been clearly defined by the harmonious coexistence of orthodox Catholics and of a heretical religious movement known as Catharism or, after one of the cities of the Languedoc, as the Albigensians. Weil recognized that it was impossible to be a follower of a religion that had been dead for centuries. Nevertheless, during her two years in the region she studied Catharism, writing a number of articles on the Cathars for the journal *Cahiers du Sud*. (The impact of the Cathars on Weil's own religious thought is a question I shall take up again in Chapter 5.)

Weil did not, however, only bury her head in books; she also made efforts to establish personal contacts in the area. In the *Cahiers du Sud* she wrote very positively about meetings of the Young Christian Workers' Movement that she attended. In these meetings her old involvement in workers' movements, and her developing religious interests, were brought together. Among these young Christians, she wrote, 'Christianity has an authentic ring; it is that which used to give to slaves a supernatural liberty.' Also in Marseilles, Weil was put in touch with a Resistance group. After she had been involved only a short time, however, an informer betrayed the group and the police came calling at the Weil family flat. She was subsequently examined by a military magistrate on several occasions, but in spite of his threats and attempt to intimidate Simone by threatening her parents, she said nothing and was released. She re-established links with the Resistance during her last months in Marseilles, when she acted for them as a courier and distributed copies of the movement's anti-fascist journal.

As important as any of her other contacts, however, was her increasing contact with practising Roman Catholics. Through a friend, Weil was introduced to Fr Perrin, a priest at the Dominican Convent in Marseilles. Gentle, ascetic, almost blind, Fr Perrin was graced with an intelligence and integrity that made him the ideal conversation partner, with whom

Weil could work through her questions about the Christian faith. Weil met him in June 1941, and when he was moved to Montpellier in March 1942 they kept in touch, meeting and writing to each other until Weil left France. It was with Perrin above all that Weil worked through her attitude to baptism. It was also for Perrin that she wrote her 'Spiritual Autobiography' (WG 29–49), which gives an account of her evolving experience of God. The conclusion Weil drew from her conversations with Fr Perrin was that though she regarded herself as a Christian, she could not be baptized into a Church that professed so many beliefs with which she could not in conscience agree. In spite of this, she later advised her brother to have his daughter baptized, and when Weil fell ill in London she hinted to a friend that if she became comatose, her friend should arrange for her to be baptized.

In August 1941 Perrin put her in touch with a devout Catholic layman, Gustave Thibon, who was a vine farmer in Saint-Marcel d'Ardèche on the river Rhône. She worked for him throughout the vine harvest. Although Thibon offered her accommodation in his home, she insisted on living in a dilapidated cottage nearby. The work was back-breaking and the working day long. Weil learned the 'Our Father' in the Greek form it took in Matthew's Gospel, and recited it each morning before work and whenever the work and her migraines became too much to bear. Sometimes during these recitations she would feel Christ present with her, 'his presence . . . infinitely more real, more moving, more clear than on that first occasion when he took possession of me' (WG 38).

The tendency towards an ascetic lifestyle had always been a feature of Weil's character. During her time in Marseilles, however, this tendency began to become more pronounced. A new friend, a ship's doctor named Bercher, was worried by this. He later noted to Fr Perrin that to Simone, eating seemed a base and disgusting function. He told her that his sister, a Benedictine nun, once recounted the story of a nun who went for a long time without eating, nourishing herself on the Eucharist alone. Weil found this story not only reasonable but something to be aspired to. In Marseilles, Weil refused to queue for rations, and often gave her own rations in packages to the prison camps where the enemies of the Nazis were being gathered by the puppet Vichy government. When a Vietnamese man she had supported brought a chicken to her as a gift, she refused to eat it with her parents and their guest.

After two years the Weil family were finally given their exit visas. The period in Vichy France had been immensely productive for Weil. Between 1940 and 1942 she had written most of the essays subsequently published in *Intimations of Christianity among the Ancient Greeks*, she had filled several notebooks (from which *Gravity and Grace* were later extracted), and had written a number of articles on science, history, literature and philosophy. Before her departure, as though she knew she was bidding farewell to her friends for the last time, she gave her notebooks to Gustave Thibon, and her 'Spiritual Autobiography' to Father Perrin. In May the Weil family went by ship to Casablanca, where they were detained in a holding camp. Simone watched with interest the religious practices of the Jews there. After a brief wait, the family boarded a ship for the USA, where they arrived on 6 July 1942.

In New York Weil continued to pester local priests about her inner dialogue concerning baptism, writing the 'Letter to a Priest' (in *Gateway to God*), which elaborated on what she had told Perrin about her doubts. Above all, Weil was desperate to gain permission to go to London to join the Free French forces. She wanted especially to gain acceptance of her plan for front-line nurses discussed earlier in this chapter. In the French Consulate in New York she met an old acquaintance, Simone Deitz, and together they explored the city, attending black churches in Harlem on Sundays. In November, having finally received the necessary permission, the two Simones began the hazardous two-week journey across a U-boat-infested Atlantic Ocean to Britain.

Because of her former left-wing sympathies it took longer than was usual for Weil to pass through the holding camp for refugees in which the British tried to weed out potential threats to national security. An old student contemporary, Maurice Schumann (later Foreign Minister in de Gaulle's government) was, fortuitously, a senior figure in the Free French. Schumann facilitated Weil's induction into London life and into the ranks of those working for the liberation of France. She took lodgings in Holland Park, West London, with a widow and her two children whom she enjoyed assisting with their homework. Weil tried, to the end, to sound an upbeat note in her letters to her parents, but her enjoyment of London and of Londoners was genuine enough:

> In the evenings people dance in the open air in the parks. The more frivolous little cockney girls go every evening to the parks and the pubs with boys whom they pick up on the way – to the great distress of their mothers, who cannot persuade them to go to church instead. (SL 199)

The indomitable humour of the British in adversity matched what she had heard of it, and she savoured the vibrant atmosphere of pub culture. Nevertheless, Weil was in London for other reasons than to enjoy herself. She continued to work at her theological studies, sleeping only a few hours a night. Her landlady worried because she ate so little, but Weil asserted that she would only eat what she took to be the rations of those in occupied France, which she considered an act of moral solidarity with her fellow French. There may well be in this a degree of rationalizing an eating disorder, but her decision was clearly of a piece with her life-long commitment to sharing others' misfortune.

Schumann found work for her at the provisional government's Ministry of the Interior in the Commissariat of action upon France. Here, her superior, Francis-Louis Closon, gave her the job of reporting on all documents coming out of

France of a political nature. Weil read and summarized reports produced by Resistance groups about the political shape of post-war France. She was well-suited for the task, but her heart was not in it. She continued to press her idea for front-line nurses, but de Gaulle rejected it. Another idea of Weil's, however, he accepted, albeit in a somewhat altered form. Weil suggested that a 'Supreme Council of the Revolt' be established in France to co-ordinate from within the movement to liberate the continent. This helped alert the Free French to the need to involve what were politically very diverse Resistance groups in political thinking as well as in disrupting the German occupying forces. Weil also asked to be parachuted into occupied France as a 'secret agent'. Her health and temperament made this impossible, as did her obviously Jewish appearance, but Weil could not see this; more to the point, she could not see that what was at issue was less that she might endanger herself than that she might endanger her colleagues. When her friend Simone Deitz was accepted for such a mission, Weil pressed her to swap places. When Deitz refused the exchange, Weil was beside herself with jealousy and only relaxed after the mission was cancelled.

It was as part of her work in the Ministry of the Interior that Weil was asked to give attention to a philosophical basis for a post-war French Constitution. This led to her essays 'On Human Personality', the 'Draft for a Statement of Human Obligations', and the book-length *The Need for Roots*. In these essays, Weil explored how conditions for a post-war society in Europe (though particularly in France) might be established. It was not sufficient, Weil believed, to expel the Nazi Germans if what replaced them was to be nothing more than a French version of the same totalitarian ideology. The vision she developed will be addressed in greater depth in Chapter 4.

Writing reports, however, was not the dangerous mission that Weil longed for. She bitterly regretted her decision to leave Vichy France where, she now believed, the chances of serving her country were better. Overwork, hunger and despondency eventually took their toll, and in April 1943 Simone Deitz found Weil prostrate with weakness in her lodgings. She was admitted to the Middlesex Hospital. Her doctor diagnosed tuberculosis, for which the cure was a rich diet, but Weil continued to refuse all but small quantities of food, repeating to medical staff what she had told her landlady, that she could not eat more food than those in occupied France. She was not short of visitors, but was not always pleased to see them. She argued with Schumann and Closon, her Free French superiors, because they would not agree to send her into France. Also, she was increasingly frustrated with the myopia of the Free French authorities, who were intent only on winning the war without any thought about what should happen afterwards. She resigned from the Free French in July.

Her condition was not in itself necessarily life-threatening, but because she was by now habituated to tiny quantities of food she was not able to take in sufficient calories to strengthen her body. She grew weak. One report suggests that a visitor to Weil's hospital bed poured water over Weil's head and pronounced the baptismal formula as she lay dying. Eventually, the medical staff at the hospital, impatient with her, and short of beds, insisted that she be moved. A place was found for her at the Grosvenor Sanatorium in Ashford, Kent. By now she was very weak indeed, though her last letter to her parents was the first of her regular correspondence to give them any indication that she was ill:

Darlings,

Very little time or inspiration for letters now. They will be short, erratic, and far between. But you have another source of consolation [a new granddaughter] ... Au revoir, darlings, Heaps and heaps of love.   (SL 201)

Weil was taken to Ashford by Mme Closon, the wife of her forgiving former superior. From her new room she could look out over the Kent fields towards France. Again, she struggled with her doctors, and refused to eat. Eventually she was unable to move at all, and she died on 24 August 1943. Three days later the Coroner recorded that she had died of

> ... cardiac failure due to myocardial and pulmonary tuberculosis. The deceased did kill and slay herself by refusing to eat whilst the balance of her mind was disturbed.

The implication that she had committed suicide made her of momentary interest to the local newspapers. One ran a story headed: 'French Professor starves herself to death'. Another carried the headline: 'Death from starvation, French Professor's curious sacrifice'. Did Simone Weil starve herself to death? Those who knew her best think the answer is no. Weil had never been a big eater, and years of privation meant that by 1943 it caused her agonizing pain to force food into her shrunken stomach. Weil understood that the food she did not eat would not be sent to France, but she believed her lack of excess was an act of spiritual sacrifice that mattered. Ultimately, the question about whether Weil's death was wilfully self-inflicted is best judged in the light of her writings, with their unique and enigmatic blend of celebration of life and self-denial.

Seven people attended her funeral. Among them were her landlady, M. and Mme Closon, Simone Deitz and Maurice Schumann. In an ironic but fitting final twist, the priest who had been asked to come missed his train and Schumann took the missal and read the funeral prayers. Weil's landlady threw a bouquet tied with a tricolour ribbon into the grave.

Difficulties in reading Weil's writings

Before beginning an account of some of Weil's thought, a few remarks about the nature of her writings and the challenges associated in reading them are helpful.

The first challenge is that during her short life Weil's interests and beliefs changed and developed. Her early immersion in classical philosophy and political theory gave way to an increasing interest in the study of religions and in theology. Nevertheless, as we have already seen, she continued to write about philosophy and politics until her death. One way to make the developments in her thought clear would be to examine her thought in chronological sequence. However, this is not the approach taken here. Instead, her ideas have been grouped into themes. For example, Chapter 4 deals with her political theory, even though some of her political writings were written earlier, and others later, in her life.

A second challenge in reading Weil's writings, and struggling to understand her ideas, is that much of what she wrote was put into notebooks. These are condensed, pithy and gnomic observations that she intended, but rarely had the chance, to develop more fully later on. Because she did not, through force of circumstances beyond her control, publish more than a fraction of what she wrote, these notebooks were the place where she worked out her ideas. In the privacy of their pages she took greater intellectual risks. Reading the volumes of her notebooks one finds her circling round the same subject again and again, like a seagull looking for food, approaching the same subject from different angles. It is also in the nature of notes that they are not intended to be final statements of belief, but sometimes merely a getting on to paper of an undeveloped thought. Consequently, Weil occasionally seems to write two statements that are in tension. One person who tried to solve such difficulties was Gustave Thibon, the farmer and friend for whom Weil picked grapes in 1941. Thibon edited the Marseilles notebooks Weil left with him in May 1942. From the notebooks he arranged passages into themes, such as 'Gravity and Grace', 'Void and Compensation', 'Detachment' etc. This edited collection, published in English under the title *Gravity and Grace*, is undoubtedly a convenient place to begin reading Weil, but it is not the notebooks in their original form (see p. 104). It is, moreover, an abridgement and arrangement by a Roman Catholic layman intent upon presenting Weil to the world as a Catholic saint in the making. Thibon thus performed an act of both service and violence to Weil's legacy: he opened the borderless steppes of Weil's thoughts to visitors, but he fenced and tamed them to do it. While it is useful to be aware of the difficulties of reading Simone Weil, they should not be taken as grounds for despair of ever understanding her. Her writings are intellectually demanding, but Weil was a gifted communicator whose prose is more often than not exquisitely fine and clear.

A third difficulty in reading Weil's writings concerns the 'mystical' dimension of her thought. What is mysticism? In daily conversation the word 'mystic' is sometimes used to describe a person with strange psychic powers. For anatomists of religious experience, however, it refers to a person whose experience has a divine or sacred significance that surpasses natural human apprehension. Religious mystics who believe they have encountered God in this way find it difficult to put their experiences into words. Weil's writings are occasionally mystical in this technical sense; that is, they fall into a recognizable genre of religious writings. Where Weil struggles to express her 'mystical' experiences of Christ, she is difficult to understand, not because she is confused but because mysticism, like fine art or poetry, is not readily subjected to rational analysis. To add to the difficulties of understanding Weil's mysticism there is one further layer of meaning we need to add: for Weil, there is a tradition of thought – beginning with Egyptian religion and extending through certain classical Greek philosophers, including Plato, through early Christianity and kept alive by a few medieval and early modern Christians – that sought above all to form a bridge between human affliction and the love of God. She occasionally termed this tradition of thought the *mystical* tradition. It was *this* mystical tradition that Weil was attempting to echo.

There are two ways in which mysticism shows through in Weil's writings. First, in those on, for example, the love of God and affliction, or on the experience of work, it becomes clear that behind her theological reflections is a personal mystical experience of affliction, or of work, that fuels her thinking. Second, there are the very rare, but important, passages where she departs from the rules of philosophy and theology and writes in an imaginative mystical style. The most striking of these is a passage written either during her last months in Paris or perhaps when she was living in Marseilles. It communicates more effectively than this chapter is able Weil's experience of God in Christ, and the way she responded to God.

He entered my room and said: 'Poor creature, you who understand nothing, who know nothing. Come with me and I will teach you things which you do not suspect.' I followed him.

He took me into a church. It was new and ugly. He led me up to the altar and said: 'Kneel down.' I said 'I have not been baptized.' He said: 'Fall on your knees before this place, in love, as before the place where lies the truth.' I obeyed.

He brought me out and made me climb up to a garret. Through the open window one could see the whole city spread out, some wooden scaffolding, and the river on which boats were being unloaded. The garret was empty, except for a table and two chairs. He bade me be seated.

We were alone. He spoke. From time to time someone would enter, mingle in the conversation, then leave again.

Winter had gone; spring had not yet come. The branches of the trees lay bare, without buds, in the cold air full of sunshine.

The light of day would arise, shine forth in splendour, and fade away: then the moon and the stars would enter through the window. And then once more the dawn would come up.

At times he would fall silent, take some bread from a cupboard, and we would share it. This bread really had the taste of bread. I have never found that taste again.

He would pour out some wine for me, and some for himself – wine which tasted of the sun and of the soil upon which this city was built.

At other times we would stretch ourselves out on the floor of the garret, and sweet sleep would enfold me. Then I would wake and drink in the light of the sun.

He had promised to teach me, but he did not teach me anything. We talked about all kinds of things, in a desultory way, as do old friends.

One day he said to me: 'Now go.' I fell down before him, I clasped his knees, I implored him not to drive me away. But he threw me out on the stairs. I went down unconscious of anything, my heart as it were in shreds. I wandered along the streets. Then I realized that I had no idea where his house lay.

I have never tried to find it again. I understood that he had come for me by mistake. My place is not in that garret. It can be anywhere – in a prison cell, in one of those middle-class drawing rooms full of knickknacks and red plush, in the waiting-room of a station – anywhere, except in that garret.

Sometimes I cannot help trying, fearfully and remorsefully, to repeat to myself a part of what he said to me. How am I to know if I remember rightly? He is not there to tell me.

I know well that he does not love me. How could he love me? And yet deep down within me something, a particle of myself, cannot help thinking, with fear and trembling, that perhaps, in spite of all, he loves me.

(N Vol. 2 638–9)

2

Weil's understanding of God

It is clear from her letters to Father Perrin early in 1942 that Simone Weil believed she had always been Christian (see p. 14). It was not the experiences in Portugal, Assisi or Solesmes that had, she thought, been her first contacts with Christianity; she had in some sense been *born* into it:

> I always adopted the Christian attitude as the only possible one. I might say that I was born, I grew up and I always remained within the Christian inspiration. (WG 29)

> From my earliest childhood I always had also the Christian idea of love for one's neighbour, to which I gave the name of justice . . .   (WG 31)

As a student Weil had considered the existence or non-existence of God to be an insoluble philosophical problem; consequently, religious questions and religious subjects simply did not feature in her earliest writings. Even after her religious experiences led her to attend to religious subjects in her notebooks, Weil's approach was refreshingly unconventional. At no time did she conceive of herself as seeking after God, and she appears to have been unconcerned with the question of her own salvation. In short, Weil's understanding of God and of what it means to live within the 'Christian inspiration' differed significantly from how a Catholic priest like Fr Perrin understood the Christian faith. Several of the Church's teachings (its 'dogma') Weil considered to be unnecessary additions to the essence of what Christianity is about:

25

Of course I knew quite well that my conception of life was Christian. That is why it never occurred to me that I could enter the Christian community. I had the idea that I was born inside. But to add dogma to this conception of life, without being forced to do so by indisputable evidence, would have seemed to me a lack of honesty.   (WG 32)

Part of her hesitancy as she stood at the door of the Church lay in a kind of dread – learned in part from the Platonic philosophy she had studied in Alain's classroom at the Lycée Henri IV – conjured up in her by certain sorts of *social structure*. The Church's faults and failings she could put up with; what worried her was the way any human group or 'collective' tended to subordinate the individual opinions of its members to the party line. Individual Nazis risked giving themselves up to the Party; patriots risked being so caught up in love of their country that they could no longer discern the justice or injustice of its actions. Just so, Weil feared losing her freedom of belief and conscience to the social structure of the Church (see WG 21–2). Plato – whose 'hero' Socrates had been forced to give up his life to the social 'collective' of Athens – called social structures 'the Great Beast'. The supreme exemplar of the Great Beast was the Roman Empire, which made force rather than justice the measure of its actions. In this respect Weil found a profound resemblance between the soul of Nazi Germany and the soul of the Roman Empire. Yet Weil borrowed the term not only to categorize nation states, but also the Church in which individual saints, otherwise true and good, were constrained by their loyalty to the Church to support evils such as the Crusades and the Inquisition. Unconditional love for the Church was, for Weil, a form of idolatry. The shoe pinched at the point where the Church abused its authority to exclude from grace those who departed from one or other aspects of its particular interpretation of Christ's life and teaching. The phrase used by the Church formally to excommunicate heretics was *anathema sit*. Weil notes:

It is the use of the two little words *anathema sit*. It is not their existence, but the way they have been employed up till now. It is that also which prevents me from crossing the threshold of the Church.　　　　　　　(WG 43)

In spite of this, when another Catholic in Marseilles challenged Weil's attitude to Church dogma and said, as a matter of factual definition, that she was a heretic, Weil was flabbergasted.

Sources for our knowledge of God

If Weil did not shape her religious convictions according to the doctrines of the Roman Catholic Church, what were the sources of her beliefs? She believed that Jesus Christ embodied deep truths – for example about the nature of human affliction and about God – but that these truths had also been present in other religious and philosophical traditions throughout human history. The choice facing her (and indeed everyone) was not therefore between being a Christian and being damned, but between truth and falsehood: '[t]here is not a Christian point of view and other points of view; there is truth and error. It is not that anything which isn't Christianity is false, but everything which is true is Christianity' (FLN 80). 'Truth' *included* Christianity, but it was not exclusive to it. On the contrary, she records in her notebook that:

It is impossible that the whole truth should not be present at every time and every place, available for anyone who desires it. 'Whoever asks for bread'. Truth is bread. It is absurd to suppose that for centuries nobody, or hardly anybody, desired the truth, and then that in the following centuries it was desired by whole peoples.　　(FLN 302)

In Weil's judgment God's truth did not first enter the world with the man Jesus, and neither has it been available since Jesus' incarnation only to Church members. Many religious traditions,

Weil thought, though they differ in outward appearance, 'agree' with the Christian Gospels in fundamental respects:

> Except in countries that have subordinated their spiritual life to imperialism, a mystic doctrine lies at the secret core of every religion; and although the mystic doctrines differ from each other, they are not only similar but absolutely identical as regards a certain number of essential points.
>
> (OL 169)

The most obvious non-Christian source of religious truth to Weil was the philosophy and literature of the ancient Greeks. For Weil, Homer's *Iliad* and the tragedies of the playwrights Aeschylus (525–456 BC) and Sophocles (*c.* 496–406 BC) 'bear the clearest indication that the poets who produced them were in a state of holiness' (NR 224). Not only are these texts works of literary genius; for Weil they contained within them the same divine truth that is present in the teaching of Jesus. In the essays of *Intimations of Christianity among the Ancient Greeks*, Weil surveyed the jewels of classical Greek literature. In Homer's *Iliad*, for example, she perceived a 'miraculous object . . . the only veritable epic of the Western world' (IC 51). She found in the *Iliad* and in other texts a series of striking parallels between Greek thought and Christian theology. Weil was not the first Christian thinker to consider the relationship between classical Greek thought and the gospel of Christ. In the third century, for example, Clement of Alexandria wrote that 'philosophy was given to the Greeks to fit their ears for the good news', suggesting thereby that Christianity was in some sense a fulfilment of the religious aspirations of the Greeks, which retained some value as a preparation for the Christian gospel. This was not, however, quite the same position as Simone Weil's. Greek thought did not, for her, pave the way to Christianity; rather it contained within it the same essential truths also contained in the Gospels.

One example, taken from many possible instances in Weil's essays, illustrates the seriousness of her suggestion. It concerns

the Greek myth of Prometheus, which was told most beauti-
fully by Aeschylus in the play *Prometheus Bound*. Prometheus
belonged to the Titans, a race of semi-divine beings des-
cended from the gods. Prometheus stole fire from heaven and,
because of his selfless love for them, he gave it to humankind.
For this crime Zeus, the chief of the gods, chained Prometheus
to a rock, where an eagle came daily to feast on his liver (which
grew back at night), until he was eventually freed.

'If one compares lines from the *Prometheus*,' wrote Weil, 'the
similarity of the story of Prometheus with that of Christ
appears with blinding evidence' (IC 58). First, she suggested,
like Christ, Prometheus suffered because of his love for
humanity. Crying in agony to heaven Prometheus shouts:

> I have delivered mortals
> from the damnation that would have flung them into Hades.
> It is for this fault that these tortures crush me. (IC 62)

As Christ was crucified for love of humanity, so Prometheus
was *crucified* (and Weil uses exactly this word) upon the rock
for the same reason.

Aeschylus also describes Prometheus as being, like Christ,
the instructor of human beings who has taught them all things
necessary for their salvation. Indeed, Prometheus describes his
suffering with the Greek word *pascho*, from which the French
word for the Passion (suffering) of Christ is taken. In *cruci-
fying* Prometheus, Weil continued, Zeus opened the way of
wisdom to humanity, for it is only through an understanding
of suffering that a true knowledge of God is possible.

In addition to the parallels between the suffering of Prometheus and Christ, and their origin in love for humanity, Weil
makes another observation concerning the relationship of Zeus
to Prometheus and of God the Father to Christ the Son. Contrary
to what the horror of the punishment might lead one to believe,
there was, she suggests, a high degree of consent and co-
operation between Zeus and Prometheus, and in this respect

their relationship mirrors that between God the Father and Jesus Christ. In Aeschylus' play, Zeus and Prometheus are said to be one. The crucifixion of Prometheus is Zeus' chosen way to give an understanding of suffering to humanity. From his rock, Prometheus says that Zeus

... Shall soften one day, when
as I have said, he shall be shattered; he, the inflexible,
he shall appease his anger; in union with me and in
    friendship
he shall hasten to me as I hasten to him.   (IC 62)

In some versions of the myth, Prometheus' case is so compelling that Zeus is eventually forced to unchain him. Weil concluded that in some mysterious way Prometheus is a part of Zeus himself, crucified on the rock. This idea – the separation of God from himself – only makes sense, Weil suggested, when it is recalled that Christ on his cross cried out that he had been abandoned by God (Matthew 27.46). At the moment of crucifixion, there is an apparent opposition between Father and Son, just as there is between Zeus and Prometheus. In the stories of Prometheus and of Christ's crucifixion there is a moment, therefore, when God is both executioner and victim, master and slave. This interpretation is reinforced when Prometheus freely acknowledges that he has accepted affliction for the sake of humanity: 'I knew all that, I consented, I have consented to take the blame' (IC 70).

In one respect, Weil acknowledged a difference between the crucifixion of Prometheus and Christ. Prometheus' sacrifice, she argued, 'never appears as a historical dated fact which might have happened at a certain point in time and at a certain place' (IC 70). Naturally, the historical events of the life and death of Jesus cannot have been known centuries earlier by Aeschylus. Thus, Weil believed, there is nothing in the comparison of these two stories that weakens in any way the distinctive historical truth of the Gospels. However, if

Christ existed before the foundation of the world as the Lamb that was slain (Revelation 13.8), then, Weil wrote: 'The story of Prometheus is like the refraction into eternity of the Passion of Christ' (IC 70); consequently the resemblances between the two stories 'can only confirm, and not weaken, the Christian dogma' (IC 71).

Weil drew similar comparisons between Christian tradition and other religious traditions. Of the living religions, she familiarized herself with Buddhist and Hindu Scriptures in particular, and drew conclusions about the presence of divine truth in them similar to those within the myth of Prometheus. She also greatly admired the Egyptian cult of Osiris and the religion of the Cathars of the Languedoc. She concluded that:

> Every time that a man has, with a pure heart called upon Osiris, Dionysus, Krishna, Buddha, the Tao etc., the Son of God has answered him by sending the Holy Spirit.
>
> (GWG 114)

Common to all of these religions (although not, in Weil's opinion, common to either Islam or Judaism) was a crucial insight that 'proved' that the divine truth was present within them. This insight was the holy beauty of suffering. For Weil, it was a proper apprehension of human and divine suffering that indicated the presence of God within a religious or philosophical tradition of thought. In a telling aphorism from her notebooks Weil goes so far as to divorce the cross of Christ from his resurrection in such a way as to privilege the significance of the former over the latter: 'Hitler,' she argued,

> could die and return to life again fifty times, but I should still not look upon him as the Son of God. And if the Gospel omitted all mention of Christ's resurrection, faith would be easier for me. The Cross by itself suffices me. For me the proof, the really miraculous thing, is the perfect beauty of the accounts of the Passion. (GWG 129)

31

It is also not difficult to understand why some of those with whom she shared her views judged them formally heretical from a Catholic point of view. It was not simply a question of whether Weil's assertion that divine truth is present in religious and philosophical traditions other than Christianity may be thought to compromise the uniqueness of Jesus Christ. Neither was it simply a question of her failing to consider the integrity of cross and resurrection in Christian teaching as two movements in a single drama, with the result that she reduces resurrection to the resuscitation of a corpse. For those, like Fr Perrin, with whom she shared her views, Weil was caught up in a tragic spiritual conflict between her attraction to Christ, the Eucharist and the gospel on the one hand, and on the other by her implacable opposition to social, philosophical and historical forces that oppressed her. Within this conflict, Weil had no authoritative source on which she could rely, other than what her own experience and opinions told her about where truth lay. The Church was 'true' in so far as it agreed with her perception of divine truth; its Scriptures were 'true' insofar as they resourced an understanding of divine truth as the perfect beauty of the Passion. She rejected Church and Bible as rules (or canons) of truth, leaving her alone with her own judgment.

The prime example of the consequences of this dilemma is Weil's fierce repudiation of the Old Testament and of Jewish faith. Weil rejected her Jewish ancestry in an excessively forthright way (see p. 3). In her notebooks she spelled out in detail what it was about the 'Jewish God' that she found so repellent. She argued that Moses, the greatest Jewish prophet but educated as an Egyptian 'prince', knew about the divine truth in other religions, but had wilfully chosen to reject it. The Hebrews, she suggested, far from understanding affliction as a gateway to God's truth, believed it to be a symptom of the sinfulness of the sufferer. Suffering was God's punishment of sinful people. With the exception of the Book of Job and a few passages in the prophets such as the songs of the suffering servant in Isaiah, Jewish Scriptures were concerned with the worship of power. She had, she wrote in a letter,

> always been kept away from Christianity by its ranking these stories, so full of pitiless cruelty, as sacred texts . . . I have never been able to understand how it is possible for a reasonable mind to regard the Jehovah of the Bible and the Father who is invoked in the Gospel as one and the same being. (SL 129–30)

The God of the Old Testament was, to Weil, a God of violence; to worship this God was to worship the force at the heart of the Great Beast.

> *Israel.* From Abraham onwards (including himself, but excepting some of the prophets), and as though it had been planned, everything becomes sullied and foul, as if to demonstrate quite clearly: Look! There it is, evil! (GG 161)

There are several sorts of problems with Weil's sweeping and hysterical assertions about Jews and Judaism. Why is it that her sensitivity to the violence and force present in the Hebrew Scriptures leads her to reject them, when she can see beyond the violence and force of the *Iliad* to the 'holiness' within it? Typically a fair and careful reader of texts, has Weil read the Hebrew Scriptures with sufficient patience and care? Typically a writer who – for example when narrating the history of Imperial Rome or Renaissance Florence – is willing to subject her interpretation of history to the discipline of historical evidence, has Weil examined the origins of Christianity without a similar willingness to abide by the evidence? When it comes to the Jewish roots of Christian thought Weil's views are puzzlingly bizarre: ignoring all evidence to the contrary, Weil argued that far from being Jewish: 'The Gospels are the last and most marvellous expression of Greek genius' (IC 52). She even speculated that the Lord's Prayer had originally been spoken by Jesus in Greek, because of the beauty of the prayer in the Greek language of the New Testament. Theologically too, Weil's repeated assertion that the God of the Old Testament and the God of the New Testament are, as it were, different Gods, is problematic for reasons that will be taken up once more in Chapter 5. But all of this – the psychologically damaged, the historically absurd, the theologically heterodox – could in an important sense be overlooked, were it not for the fact that her thinking is unfolding at the same time as the Shoah, the destruction of the Jews also known as the Holocaust. Simone Weil, who set her face against injustice, turns it from the defining injustice of the century being enacted upon European Jews. Weil, whose reflections are at their most profound when teasing out the threads that bind God to human suffering, is blinded by her febrile anti-Judaism to the presence of God behind the wire of concentration camp and gas chamber. It is beside the point, in this regard, that Weil's analysis of the rise of Nazism failed to penetrate to the central core of anti-Semitism in Nazi policy and practice, or to remark that the full impact of Nazi anti-Semitism was not apparent in Vichy France before she left it in 1943, and that she is consequently not culpable for failing to confront it. Weil's failure is not one of critical analysis or of knowledge, so much as it is a failure to register that the pathos of Israel's journey with God – a pathos that had been echoed on the cross of Jesus Christ and was now being echoed in the Shoah – was in some sense her own.

God's existence

In rejecting Judaism Weil was neglecting profound resonances between some of her own thinking and that of Jewish thought. Nowhere is this more obvious than in her wrestling with what she called 'the necessary non-existence of God'. In simple terms, responses to the question of God's existence fall into three categories: theism (belief in God), atheism (rejection of belief in God), and agnosticism (belief that the existence or non-existence of God cannot be known with certainty). To Weil, however, these categories misrepresent the complexity of God's existence. It is not possible to speak of God's existence, she argued, without eventually coming up against contradictions. Weil was not at all worried by this; indeed she believed that contradictions can sometimes be immensely fruitful. When the intellect is confronted by apparently conflicting ideas, patient reflection upon them may yield powerful insights into truth, since 'impossibility is the door of the supernatural' (GG 95). An obvious example is the doctrine of the Trinity: God is one, and God is three persons. Another example is the mystery of the cross, which is both Christ's self-giving and his punishment.

For Weil, God's existence too can also be expressed as a contradiction:

> A case of contradictories which are true. God exists: God does not exist. Where is the problem? I am quite sure that there is a God in the sense that I am quite sure my love is not illusory. I am quite sure that there is not a God in the sense that I am quite sure nothing real can be anything like what I am able to conceive when I pronounce this word. But that which I cannot conceive is not an illusion. (GG 114)

What does Weil mean by saying that nothing real can correspond to what we imagine when we say the word 'God'? Weil recognized that human needs are incredibly powerful. So powerful is our need to be loved, for example, that we distort the reality of the beloved so that they match our needs. The person we love may not love us, but we want them to so much that we imagine our feelings are reciprocated. Instead of loving someone for who they are, we love them as who we would like them to be. This represents a flaw in the human imagination that can also occur when we try to imagine God. When we imagine God, how can we know that we are not conjuring up a false picture simply because of the force of our need for a particular kind of god? Weil's answer is that we cannot know. The only solution is to let go of imagining God's existence altogether, and to let God be

God. A soul without grace inevitably makes God into an object, while a graced soul refrains from speaking of God because the action of grace has dissolved the 'I' that would speak of God as something separate from itself. For this reason, Weil can say that:

> Of two men who have no experience of God, he who denies him is perhaps nearer to him than the other. The false God who is like the true one in everything, except that we cannot touch him, prevents us from ever coming to the true one. We have to believe in a God who is like the true God in everything, except that he does not exist, since we have not yet reached the point where God exists.   (GG 115)

Weil's argument might lead us in several directions. One direction might be to become so frustrated with the impossibility of speaking of God that we give up talking about him altogether. But Weil does not draw this conclusion from her own arguments. Far from excluding contemplation of God's truth, awareness of the contradiction of God's existence opens up the possibility of genuine attention to God. To say that we cannot speak of God as if he is an object in the world of things is therefore not the last thing that can be said about God's existence, but is, rather, one moment in a process the end point of which is the true God in whom I place my whole life and hope.

If Weil is right, for example, that it is impossible to speak about God without making God into what we want him to be in our imaginations, then the limitations of dogma as the basis of faith begin to become clear. Jesus said: 'Not everyone who says to me "Lord, Lord", will enter the kingdom of heaven, but only one who does the will of my Father in heaven' (Matthew 7.21). Weil argued that there is no value in thinking that just because we believe in a particular doctrine, for example that Jesus is Lord, we have achieved anything. Weil concluded that:

> The dogmas of the faith are not things to be affirmed. They are things to be regarded from a certain distance, with attention, respect and love. They are like the bronze

serpent [cf. Numbers 21.8–9] whose virtue is such that whoever looks upon it shall live. This attentive and loving gaze, by a shock on the rebound, causes a source of light to flash on the soul which illuminates all aspects of human life on this earth. Dogmas lose this virtue as soon as they are affirmed. (GWG 125–6)

Thus, the only legitimate response to religious mysteries in the Christian tradition or in any other tradition, is not to affirm doctrines, but to love God. The truly important religious question is not 'Are you saved?' or 'Do you believe in God?' but 'Do you love God with the whole of your attention?'

One feature of Weil's proposals about loving God remains particularly difficult to grasp. Weil had argued that we must let go of God's existence, since it is impossible to hold God in our imaginations without distorting him. But if God cannot be imagined, if dogmas about God are intrinsically limited, how do we know what God is like in order to love him? How do we know that God is like a loving Father and not merely some malicious super-being? Weil argued, as we have seen, that we are to 'believe in a God who is like the true God in everything, except that he does not exist'. However, for Weil this does not mean that we cannot say anything about God. Drawing on an insight of the eighteenth-century philosopher Immanuel Kant, Weil recalls a lesson to be learned from comparing one hundred real pound coins and one hundred imaginary pound coins. There are some differences between them; one can spend the real coins but not the imaginary ones, for instance. However, we can say some things about the imaginary coins and still make perfect sense. Even though they are imaginary, there are still exactly one hundred coins, not one pound more, not one less. In an analogous way, Weil believed that we can still truthfully say certain things about the God who cannot be conceived as existing: the God who cannot be conceived as an object of thought may nonetheless be said to be good, just and loving. Weil noted:

> Nothing which exists is absolutely worthy of love. We must therefore love that which does not exist. This non-existent object of love is not a fiction, however, for our fictions cannot be any more worthy of love than we ourselves, and we are not worthy of it. (GG 110)

Thus, even though Weil insisted that we must believe in God as though he does not exist, we can still *genuinely* love him. It is thus in the light of Weil's rejection of dogma, and her redefinition of faith as attentive love towards God, that proper meaning can be made of the affirmation that Weil made in her last months to a friend, that she believed in God, in the Trinity, in the incarnation, in the redemption, and in the teachings of the Gospels.

Waiting on God

Weil established that the proper aim of someone seeking God is not belief, but attention. What Weil meant by attention, however, is not immediately obvious. The French word Weil uses (*attente*) conveys the sense both of attention and of waiting. What Weil attempted to communicate with the concept is both an attitude of readiness to God, and a kind of patient non-activity. The purest form of this attention, for Weil, is prayer; indeed:

> Attention, taken to its highest degree, is the same thing as prayer. It presupposes faith and love ... Absolutely unmixed action is prayer. (GG 117)

Such attentiveness to God has widespread ramifications for daily life:

> [It] makes certain things impossible for us. Such is the non-acting action of prayer in the soul. There are ways of behaviour which would veil such attention should they be indulged in and which, reciprocally, this attention puts out of the question. (GG 119)

One such pattern of behaviour precluded by a life of attention to God is excessive attachment to this world. While 'non-

38

attachment' to the world is a prominent feature of many religious traditions, Weil believed that in the Christian tradition this kind of prayerful life had been kept alive only by mystics, such as St John of the Cross (1540–91). Weil believed strongly that 'detachment' should be an essential component of all Christian faith. Detachment is 'non-active' in that it does not seek the fulfilment of any personal need, but involves emptying oneself of all desire. Detachment means, for Weil,

> to empty desire, finality of all content, to desire in the void, to desire without any wishes. To detach our desire from all good things and to wait. Experience proves that this waiting is satisfied. It is then we touch the absolute good. (GG 13)

As with her theology of the existence and non-existence of God, there is a contradiction present in the notion of detachment from desire as the way to achieve fulfilment:

> We can only possess what we renounce; what we do not renounce escapes from us. In this sense, we cannot possess anything whatever unless it passes through God. (GG 34)

Weil thought that a fundamental dilemma of human existence is that on the one hand we are driven by our needs, but on the other hand, our needs are never actually satisfied. On the simplest level, for instance, we are hungry so we eat, but our satisfaction is only ever temporary, and soon we become hungry again. Even in more important matters, it is human nature never to be completely satisfied. A person may want a particular job, get it, and soon after want another, better job. This merry-go-round of desire gets in the way of attentiveness to God. Even on a more mundane level it means that most people expend themselves seeking for something that can never actually be achieved. This is an invidious situation and results in most people being very unhappy part of the time, and partly unhappy all of the time. It is to this end that the art of detachment is so crucial in achieving a genuine attentiveness to God. Just as in relation to the existence of God the believer must adopt the strategy of emptying the imagination of the existence of God, so with prayerful attention they must adopt the strategy of emptying themselves of desire.

Weil's theology of detachment may appear at first to be a technique or method, through which a person may attain God by exercising acquired skills in prayerful attentiveness. 'Weil suggests,' this interpretation might say, 'that if you follow these steps you will achieve perfect happiness.' However, Weil did *not* intend the process of detachment to be a step-by-step guide to the knowledge of God and the attainment of personal happiness. Part of what is meant by giving up one's desires, she believed, is giving up even the desire for personal salvation. Weil also maintained that because God is separated from us by an infinity of space and time, there is nothing that human beings can do to take even one step towards God:

> We cannot take a single step towards the heavens. God crosses the universe and comes to us.
>
> Over the infinity of time and space, the infinitely more infinite love of God comes to possess us. He comes at his own time. We have the power to consent to receive him or to refuse. (WG 91)

Weil makes it crystal clear that our waiting on God cannot bring God one step closer, for the coming of God is a *gift*. What the believer offers by her attentiveness is simply her consent to God's presence.

The principle of non-attachment to personal desire and to the world was, Weil believed, an essential characteristic of faith in many traditions though particularly in Buddhism (it is no coincidence that at the same time Weil was developing these thoughts in Marseilles, she was also studying Buddhist Scriptures). Weil, however, developed the concept further and went on to speak of *decreation* of the self in attentiveness to God.

The initiative for this, Weil believed, came from God himself, who renounced his power in creation, and even his existence, to die on a cross. Just as God is emptied of divinity in the abandonment of Christ on the cross, so should the believer, Weil continued, renounce herself in order to respond to God. In the Eucharist, she adds, God goes so far as to be *consumed* by the believer, and invites the believer to reciprocate by offering his being to be consumed by God.

> God gave me being in order that I should give it back to
> him.   (GG 40)

> Except the seed die [cf. John 12.24] ... It has to die in
> order to liberate the energy it bears within it so that with
> this energy new forms may be developed. So we have to
> die in order to liberate a tied up energy, in order to pos-
> sess an energy which is free and capable of understand-
> ing the true relationship of things.   (GG 35)

Does decreation mean then that a believer's aim is to *eliminate* her own unique self, to wipe out her individuality as far as humanly possible? This important question is not easy to answer. It is certainly true that there are passages in Weil's notebooks in which she writes of the self, or the 'I' as she sometimes calls it, as something to be overridden.

> The sin in me says 'I' ... It is because of my wretched-
> ness that I am 'I'.   (GG 30)

> The self is only the shadow which sin and error cast by
> stopping the light of God, and I take this shadow for a
> being.   (GG 40)

However, this was not, for Weil, the same thing as believing that the self is something *bad*. For her, the natural desires of the self get in the way of God. Weil was careful to distinguish decreation of the self, and destruction of the self. To destroy something meant to make it cease to exist, to become nothing. Decreating the self, however, meant transforming it from something that belonged to the natural world, into something that belonged to God. Decreation was a continuation of the phrase in the Lord's Prayer that asks that 'Thy will be done'. She hoped that by means of decreation, her own needs would cease to get in the way of God's love for the world:

> If only I knew how to disappear there would be a perfect union of love between God and the earth I tread, the sea I hear . . . May I disappear in order that those things that I see may become perfect in their beauty from the very fact that they are no longer things that I see.   (GG 42)

As I suggested in Chapter 1, mysticism is by its nature difficult to comprehend. Weil's understanding of attention and waiting on God, and their practice through detachment and decreation of the self, are not to be approached as if they were simply abstract intellectual proposals: Weil suggests we may only apprehend what it means to efface oneself, to become detached from oneself and one's desires, to decreate the 'I' and become transparent to the love of God, if we approach God with the whole of our attention. Such attention is a form of prayer. In this sense such reflections are not intended as subjects for discussion, but for practice. Weil once observed:

> Human thought and the universe constitute the books of revelation *par excellence*, if the attention, lighted by love and faith, knows how to decipher them. The reading of them is a proof, and indeed the only certain proof. After having read the *Iliad* in Greek, no one would dream of wondering whether the professor who taught him the Greek alphabet had deceived him.   (IC 201)

The only way to 'prove' the value of Weil's 'grammar' of the spiritual life is to become attentive to God, to detach oneself from the world, and to decreate one's own ego.

3

Loving God in a world full of pain

For anyone who experiences suffering or who thinks about the suffering of others, one profound question becomes insistent: Why must people suffer? For those who believe in God, the question is even more urgent. If God is powerful and loving, why does he allow people to suffer? Is it because he is not all-powerful? Is it because he is not, after all, a loving God, and allows suffering or, worse still, causes it to happen out of malice or whimsy? As Weil observed, the question 'Why?' is so inevitable as a reaction to suffering that on the cross even Christ himself asked it: 'My God, my God, why have you forsaken me?' If we are to love God then it is vital that we find a way of coming to terms with this question.

The law of gravity

Weil identified a major obstacle that gets in the way of a proper understanding of suffering. She considered that the perception most people have of the world is so corrupt, base and superficial that, confronted with suffering, they cannot see beyond their own experience to the wider view necessary to resolve the question. The first step towards coming to terms with suffering, Weil believed, is to understand something about the forces that press upon the human soul; that is, about the nature and reality of this world. In order to describe the condition of human life, and the reality of the world, Weil used two particularly demanding concepts: *gravity* and *necessity*. Before examining the first of these, it is useful to recall Weil's life-long fascination with mathematics and science.

It is said that above the door of his Academy the philosopher Plato had inscribed the words: 'Let no one ignorant of mathematics enter here.' This was a sentiment that Weil entirely agreed with. For her, the insights afforded by philosophy and theology were inextricably interwoven with the insights of mathematics and science. A note written in New York suggests the intimacy, for Weil, of the relation of mystical truth and geometry: 'The key is harmony . . . Christ is the key. All geometry proceeds from the cross' (FLN 98). Thus, Weil's notebooks are peppered with algebraic formulae, and with mathematical diagrams that illustrate her thought. It seemed perfectly sensible for Weil to translate what she knew about geometry, physics or biological science into her own philosophical writings. One way she did this was by means of *analogy*; that is, by observing the agreement or similarity between certain specific characteristics of the laws of science and the 'laws' of the human soul and the realities of human life. In one sense, Weil's analogies involve nothing more than drawing illustrations from the world of science and employing them like a poet might employ a metaphor – to bring colour and clarity to her philosophical argument. However, occasionally she uses an analogy so frequently and consistently that it seems as though she intended more than a poetic comparison. Her use of the terms gravity and necessity fall into this second pattern.

One of the most important of the analogies Weil used was her comparison of the laws of gravity and the laws that govern the inner life of the human soul:

All the *natural* movements of the soul are controlled by laws analogous to those of physical gravity.   (GG 1)

Each person who has not turned towards God, she argued, far from being a free agent – able to choose who they are and what they do – is subject to laws of the soul, just as a falling stone is subject to the laws of physical gravity. (In French, Weil uses the word *pesanteur* for gravity, which can also mean 'heaviness' or 'sluggishness'.) 'The law of gravity,' she maintained, 'which is sovereign on earth over all material motion is the image of the carnal attachment which governs the tendencies of the soul' (SNLG 151). Unless God intervenes, this moral law of gravity determines the behaviour of the soul and makes it behave in predictable ways. Gravity, for example, is the reason why, when someone needs us, one of our natural reactions is to pull away; our soul reacts as if pushed by an unseen force as powerful as the force of gravity (we might query here whether Weil is right to extrapolate from her own experience of human relationships a universal law of human reactions to love?). When her headaches were particularly violent, Weil noted, she longed intensely for others to experience the same suffering as herself. This too, she believed, was evidence of the force of gravity on her soul. It is gravity that forces the soul to conform to society's values and needs instead of paying attention to God.

The natural impulse of the soul to behave in such ways was, for Weil, similar to what theologians might describe as a tendency of human beings to sin. Although she never wrote that human subjection to moral gravity was identical to behaving immorally, Weil made it clear that to be unthinkingly obedient to the impulses of human nature is to commit a great sin.

However, just as gravity was not the only physical law governing physical life on the planet, moral gravity was, to Weil, not the only law governing the life of the human soul. In addition to the law of gravity that causes the soul to sink into corruption, there is another force that leads it to God:

Two forces rule the universe: light and gravity.　(GG 1)

The only force powerful enough to overcome the effects of physical gravity is solar energy. In a frequently repeated image,

Weil described how the force of *grace* operates on the soul like light on a plant. Imagine the life of a seed that germinates beneath a heavy slab of concrete. The force of gravity presses down on the concrete, which in turn presses down on to the plant. However, miraculously, the young plant is so attracted to the sun that it is able to find its way through the smallest crack in the concrete, and grow upwards into the light. Thus, the force of light is able to defeat the laws of gravity as light is transformed into the energy that enables the plant to grow. Human beings cannot help having the natural impulses Weil describes as moral gravity, but they can choose to be blindly obedient to them, or to reach towards God like a plant grows towards light.

Weil pressed this analogy even further. *All* energy on earth, she continued, comes either directly or indirectly from the sun. Plants transform the energy contained within light, and store it. This energy enters into animals when plants are eaten. Alternatively, the energy is stored in wood, coal or oil. Thus, the direct energy of the sun is buried and hidden until it is dug up and burned as fuel. Weil proposed that this summary of the nature of energy 'is the image of grace, which comes down to be buried in the darkness of our souls and is the only source of energy which can counteract the trend towards evil which is the moral law of gravity' (SNLG 151).

Grace, like energy, cannot be taken, only received. All a farmer can do, she added, is to arrange his farm in such a way that his animals and plants can receive this energy. In a similar way, no one can go out and take grace – all they can do is to so dispose their souls that they may be able to receive the gift of grace. To 'tilt' the soul towards the light, however, involves first of all acknowledging that it is subject to gravity. Not everyone achieves this. Most people live in the world dominated by their shallow sensations without ever realizing that they are subject to the unseen force of moral gravity.

Necessity and obedience

The second difficult but crucial concept Weil used was that of *necessity*. Weil characterized necessity in two apparently contradictory ways. On the one hand, necessity represented for Weil the pitiless harshness of life in the world. On the other hand, necessity was the reality of God's world, calling us to be obedient to him. Let us consider first what Weil meant by describing the relentless harshness of the world as necessity.

The world is changing all the time. However, Weil argued, there are certain things about the world that in spite of its changing remain consistent. One of these is its continual presence. The reality of the world is something we can never escape except by death. 'Necessity' is the name Weil gave to this characteristic of reality, its 'continual presence'. Weil knew that one common Christian understanding of the world is that after creation, God continues to be involved in the world by means of his *providence*; that is, that God cares for and protects his creatures in their life in the world. However, for Weil, this understanding is fraught with difficulties. If we believe in God's providence why, we must ask, does he seem sometimes to protect some of his creatures from harm, while at other times they are given up to suffering? When a child is suffering with cancer, for example, why should their healing be seen as God's providential intervention, while a child in the next hospital bed goes on to die? Weil's explanation is that God does not act providentially in the world at all. On the contrary:

> God abandons our entire being – flesh, blood, sensibility, intelligence, love – to the pitiless necessity of matter and the cruelty of the devil, except for the eternal and supernatural part of the soul. The Creation is an abandonment. In creating what is other than Himself, God necessarily abandoned it. He only keeps under his care

the part of Creation which is Himself – the uncreated
part of every creature.   (FLN 103)

On the cancer ward, the death of one child and the survival
of the other have nothing to do with God's providence,
according to Weil, but both result from the necessity of creation. Creation is not, she thought, 'good' (as the Book of
Genesis suggests), but neither is it bad – it is simply necessary. For Weil, therefore, the first step in coming to terms with
the 'Why?' of suffering is to understand that the question is
unanswerable. There is no divine plan hidden behind the joys
and sufferings of our life, as Christians have traditionally
affirmed. Thus, 'There can be no answer to the "Why?" of
the afflicted, because the world is necessity and not purpose'
(GWG 101).

To elaborate on this idea, Weil cited one of the sayings of
Jesus (Matthew 5.45): 'The sun shines on the just and on the
unjust . . . God makes himself *necessity*: There are two aspects
of necessity: it is exercised, it is endured: the sun and the cross'
(GG 43). Just as the sun shines on men and women irrespective of their moral qualities, so too does the rain fall upon
them. Good and bad happen to us not for a purpose, but
because the mechanism of necessity is blind. To Weil, a
crucial insight is that sun and rain, affliction and joy, come
equally from God. Thus, she argued, 'It is in his Providence
that God has willed that necessity should be like a blind
mechanism' (WG 67).

Yet the death of one child and survival of the other, Weil
wants to add, is not at all arbitrary or malicious. Such experience is simply the *necessity* of human life. One consequence
of this is that while the question 'Why?' is inevitable for those
who suffer, ultimately it is a question that cannot be answered:

> There is a question which is absolutely meaningless and
> therefore, of course, unanswerable, and which we norm-
> ally never ask ourselves, but in affliction the soul is

constrained to speak it incessantly like a sustained monotonous groan. This question is: Why? Why are things as they are? The afflicted man naïvely seeks an answer, from men, from things, from God, even if he disbelieves in him, from anything or everything . . . If one explained to him the causes which have produced his present situation, and this is in any case seldom possible because of the complex interaction of circumstances, it will not seem to him to be an answer. For his question 'Why?' does not mean 'By what cause?' but 'For what purpose?'   (GWG 100)

The value of this aspect of necessity is, therefore, that it is an image by which the mind can conceive the indifference and the impartiality of God. However, there was, for Weil, a second way of regarding necessity, and that is to love it:

One must tenderly love the harshness of that necessity which is like a coin with two faces, the one turned towards us being domination and the one turned towards God, obedience. We must embrace it closely even if it offers its roughest surface and the roughness cuts into us. Any lover is glad to clasp tightly some object belonging to an absent loved one, even to the point where it cuts into the flesh. We know that this universe is an object belonging to God.   (SNLG 196)

To Weil, though no one can choose to opt out of the world that is governed by necessity, people do have a choice about how they react to it. Weil believed that just as the laws of mathematics come from God, so too does necessity. The choice facing each person is whether or not they will submit to necessity, or strain fruitlessly against it:

We have to consent to be subject to necessity and to act only by handling it . . . Obedience is the supreme virtue. We have to love necessity.   (GG 43–4)

Sometimes, obeying this mechanism of necessity fits in naturally with our own immediate needs. When we are hungry, for instance, our obedience to necessity means satisfying our hunger by eating. However, sometimes obedience to necessity means transcending our first instinctive desires. Weil illustrated this point vividly:

> If my eternal salvation were on this table in the form of an object and if I only had to stretch out my hand to grasp it, I would not stretch out my hand without having received orders to do so. (GG 44–5)

As with the light that can lead one out from the heaviness of the moral law of gravity, so too with obedience to necessity: it cannot ever be taken, it can only ever be received as a gift. As an illustration, Weil recalled Jesus' saying about the lilies of the field (Matthew 6.28), which are more beautiful than King Solomon in all his glory, although they make no effort other than to be docile in their submission to natural necessity. To Weil, once the impartiality of God-given necessity is accepted, the beauty of the world begins to shine through:

> The beauty of the world appears when we recognise that the substance of the universe is necessity and that the substance of necessity is obedience to a perfectly wise Love. The universe of which we are a fraction has no other essence than to be obedient. (GWG 90)

Weil's solution to the difficulties of the traditional Christian theology of providence is highly original. Moreover, Weil rightly acknowledges that even if God can be described as 'abandoning' creation to the blind laws of necessity, he is still, as its creator, responsible for those laws. Even if we accept, therefore, that impartial necessity leads some to suffer and others to happiness, some way must still be found of loving the God who creates a world in which affliction occurs. Weil's proposal about how this is possible is one of her best-known and important contributions to religious thought.

The love of God and affliction

Weil's analysis of these questions used the word *malheur* – meaning not merely unhappiness or sorrow, but affliction – a condition compounded of pain and distress. Weil began by making an important distinction between *suffering* and *affliction*.

Affliction, Weil argued, 'is inseparable from physical suffering and yet quite distinct' (WG 77). It is perfectly possible, she wrote, to experience suffering without experiencing affliction. Take the example of toothache. At the time one experiences toothache, it can be excruciatingly painful. However, an hour or two after it has been fixed, it is easily forgotten; it leaves no mark on the soul. Suffering of physical pain on its own causes neither degradation nor hopelessness. Affliction, on the other hand, reaches deep down inside the soul. It is, she wrote,

> . . . an uprooting of life, a more or less attenuated equivalent of death, made irresistibly present to the soul by the attack or immediate apprehension of physical pain. If there is complete absence of physical pain there is no affliction for the soul, because our thoughts can turn to no matter what object . . . Here below physical pain, and that alone, has the power to chain down our thoughts . . .
> (WG 77)

But, it might be objected, there are many terrible human experiences that apparently have no element of physical pain and yet are profoundly hurtful to the soul. To Weil, this was quite true. However, her definition of 'physical pain' included several kinds of experience in which the body is outwardly undamaged. To Weil, for example, fear of torture should be regarded as causing physical pain, even though the body remains untouched. Similarly, when a loved one dies, even though there is no bodily wound, the grief that follows is experienced as though it were a physical pain, with difficulty in breathing, a sensation of unfulfilled need, even of hunger for the person who has been lost. Furthermore, when simple physical pain extends over a long time, its repetitive recurrence can lead the soul into genuine affliction. To Weil, this insight was clear from her own debilitating migraine headaches.

For Weil, then, the defining characteristic of affliction is that it is total. There is not real affliction 'unless the event which has seized and uprooted a life attacks it . . . in all its parts, social, psychological and physical' (WG 78).

To a person in the grip of genuine affliction, God seems absent, the soul is filled with horror as it is flung an infinite distance from God, and time stretches on ahead filled with nothing but interminable pain. To Weil, such affliction is so horrific that the soul would rather escape from affliction than death. In the light of this description, one truth about affliction becomes crystal clear:

> It is wrong to desire affliction; it is against nature, and it is a perversion; and moreover it is the essence of affliction that it is suffered unwillingly.   (GWG 87–8)

Total affliction, Weil believed, is rarer than one might imagine. To be created does not necessarily expose us to affliction, but only to its possibility. Most instances of suffering carry within them seeds of consolation. To be genuine affliction, suffering must be pure and unmitigated. Thus, for example, Weil believed that the early Christian martyrs who drew consolation in their tortures from the hope of salvation after death were not truly experiencing affliction, for their suffering was consoled by the possibility of reward. Those who suffer on behalf of a cause have their suffering mitigated because there is meaning in their suffering. In contrast, the cross of Christ, which was always Weil's model for affliction, was a criminal's death, not that of a martyr, and was characterized not by its meaning but by the fact that Jesus was exposed to ridicule. His affliction, she was convinced, was not mitigated by the knowledge that he would rise again; it was total, and his final cry – 'It is finished' – were the last words of a hopeless dying man.

Weil's description of affliction is all-encompassing. It is all the more startling therefore, when, in a letter to Joë Bousquet, a friend who was paralysed as a result of a wound received during the First World War, Weil described his afflicted state as 'privileged' and 'fortunate'. If affliction is so terrible, why on earth should one regard anyone as privileged who is forced to experience it? Weil's answer is that the privilege of affliction lies not in any intrinsic value, but in the fact that the truth of Christianity consists in a proper understanding of it. It would be a monstrous misrepresentation of God to assert that he causes affliction, even if he does so in order to teach humankind some eternal truth. To Weil, suffering was plainly evil, and consequently 'affliction in itself contains no gift from above' (GWG 95). Nevertheless, she maintained that 'knowledge of affliction is the key of Christianity' (GWG 91).

The first reason that affliction may be spoken of as a privilege is that when accepted obediently it is a way of encountering the reality of the world's necessity. Imagine greeting a close friend whom we have not seen for a long time. On meeting them, the friend grips our hand so tightly that it causes pain. However, Weil suggested, our reaction to this pain is to be glad of it, for the painful handshake confirms to us the reality of the friend's presence. Similarly, affliction, when it pierces the soul, signals an experience in which a true encounter is taking place with creation and the creator. It is only for this reason and in this spirit that it is to be welcomed.

Affliction enables a person to participate in the affliction of the world and of people within it. In her letter to Bousquet Weil wrote:

> You are specially privileged in that the present state of
> the world is a reality for you . . . you are infinitely priv-
> ileged, because you have war permanently lodged in your
> body . . . To think affliction, it is necessary to bear it in
> one's flesh, driven very far in like a nail, and for a long
> time, so that thought may have time to grow strong
> enough to regard it.   (SL 136–7)

Our natural instinct is always to flee from affliction. The feel-
ing of revulsion towards affliction is so extreme that the
afflicted person will usually turn inwards upon themselves to
escape from it. However, in the middle of the Second World
War, Weil believed that Bousquet was privileged because the
experience of the horror of war was imprinted upon his suffering body. The experience of pain, she continued, is the pain
of the universe entering the body. Weil recalled how, in the
factory, when an apprentice suffered a minor injury, the more
experienced workers would comment that the wound was the
trade entering the apprentice's body. Most people are taken
completely unawares by their affliction, they are crushed by it
and have no opportunity to come to terms with it, or to allow
it to become a part of their understanding of the world.
Bousquet, however, had the 'opportunity and the function of
knowing the truth of the world's affliction and contemplat-
ing its reality' (SL 137). It is only by learning to understand
affliction in this way that one can have a proper understanding of the affliction of others.

A second reason why affliction is the key to Christianity is
that as well as being necessary in order to enter into the suffering of others, it is also the way by which we may enter into
the suffering of God:

> Affliction is truly at the centre of Christianity . . . What
> we are commanded to love first of all is affliction: the
> affliction of man, the affliction of God.   (GWG 96)

Weil believed that in God's willingness to submit to affliction in Jesus lay the most important truth about his love for the world. Returning to the classic problem of evil, she wrote:

Either God is not almighty or he is not absolutely good, or else he does not command everywhere where he has the power to do so.

Thus the existence of evil here below, far from disproving the reality of God is the very thing which reveals him in his truth. (WG 102)

The truth about God is that he not only invites human beings to submit to necessity, in his great love he also gives himself completely to it. Jesus' crucifixion is an act of supreme obedience. On the cross, God suspends his power by an act of voluntary restraint, renouncing himself. Weil's conclusion is that there is suffering in the world not because God lacks the power to change it, or the goodness to desire that it be changed. The universe was never intended by God to be a place where he could exercise his powers; rather, God deliberately restrains himself from acting there. It is only by experiencing personal affliction that this truth about God becomes clear to us, and only then do we reach towards a proper understanding of the nature of God's love. It is in affliction that we learn to *decreate* (see Chapter 2) our own perspective, and learn how to see things from God's point of view. Such insight is ultimately a gift from God.

In one of the most important and memorable comments in her notebooks Weil summarized what she was trying to say with her theology of affliction: 'The extreme greatness of Christianity lies in the fact that it does not seek a supernatural remedy for suffering but a supernatural use for it' (GG 81). Knowledge of Christianity involved, for Weil, not deliverance from suffering but the realization that through pure affliction it is possible to meet with the immensity of God's love.

It is important to note that although Weil saw affliction as a key to Christianity, it was not her intention to diminish the horror of affliction or, indeed, of evil. Weil understood that one response to affliction is total disillusionment with the world. Faced with the presence of affliction in the world one might say not only that God is a wicked deception (since no good God could allow affliction) but also that there is nothing of ultimate value in the world since everything that is is vulnerable and fragile. However, Weil contended that if nothing in the world was of any value, then evil could not exist, since it would have nothing to take from us. Since we feel affliction to be evil, then plainly there are things of value in the world. For this reason, the greater the joy we have known, the greater will be the experience of affliction when it is lost. Thus, between evil, suffering and sin, Weil perceived a complex interrelationship:

> Evil is neither suffering nor sin; it is both at the same time, it is something common to them both. For they are linked together; sin makes us suffer and suffering makes us evil, and this indissoluble complex of suffering and sin is the evil in which we are submerged against our will and to our horror. (GWG 76)

Although affliction must under no circumstance be sought out, not even in order to experience God, nevertheless it is necessary to be as prepared to experience pure affliction as it is to be prepared for pure joy. Weil wrote to Bousquet:

> I am convinced that affliction on the one hand, and on the other hand joy, when it is a complete and pure commitment to perfect beauty, are the only two keys which give entry to the realm of purity, where one can breathe: the home of the real. (SL 141)

What unites these two keys to knowledge of God is that 'each of them must be unmixed: the joy without a shadow of incompleteness, the affliction completely unconsoled' (SL 141). Both joy and pain can be infernal, both joy and pain can be healing, both joy and pain can be celestial: it is not that joy and pain are opposed to each other, but types of joy and types of pain.

Certainly, one may find scattered throughout Weil's writings the insight that the way to God lies equally along the paths of pure joy and pure affliction. Yet, disturbingly, Weil's overwhelming emphasis is on affliction. It might be possible to defend this imbalance in her writings on the basis that she is correcting what she believed to be an extensive history of misunderstanding of affliction in Christian theology. But such a defence fails to be entirely satisfactory. Despite all her protestations to the contrary, Weil leaves her readers much less clear about the ways joy leads to God than about the ways affliction leads to God. Her attention to the ways God allows himself to be consumed, and thereby decreated in the bread and wine of the sacrament, mutes the note of thanksgiving that is the meaning of *eucharist*. Likewise, Weil's theological reserve towards the resurrection ('The Cross by itself suffices me' (GWG 129)) is symptomatic of the underdevelopment of her theology of joy compared with her theology of affliction. This is brought home in one of Weil's notebooks in which she wrote an extraordinary prayer expressing to God her complete acceptance of the possibility of affliction for herself:

> Father, in the name of Christ grant me this. That I may be unable to will any bodily movement, or any attempt at movement, like a total paralytic. That I may be incapable of receiving any sensation, like someone who is completely blind, deaf and deprived of all the senses. That I may be unable to make the slightest connection between two thoughts, even the simplest . . . And let me be a paralytic – blind, deaf, witless and utterly decrepit.
> (FLN 243–4)

The absence of a parallel prayer expressing her preparedness for total joy is emblematic of her unwillingness to make the journey from Good Friday to Easter Day.

Forms of the implicit love of God

In affliction, Weil believed, lay the key to understanding the graciousness of God's love. God submitted himself to affliction in an act of such tremendous love that it invites a response of love from human beings. However, Weil argued that direct love of God was impossible, for 'God is not present to the soul and never yet has been so' (WG 95). But though *direct* love of God is impossible, *indirect* love of God is possible by loving certain provisional, natural realities. This indirect love Weil called the implicit love of God. Weil suggested that there are three ways in which God can be loved implicitly:

> The implicit love of God can only have three immediate objects, the only three things here below in which God is really though secretly present. These are religious ceremonies, the beauty of the world and our neighbour.
>
> (WG 95)

In addition, Weil believed friendship was a form of implicit love of God that could be distinguished from that of love for our neighbour. Such forms of the implicit love for God, though veiled, are far from being poor second-bests. For the majority of people, direct love of God is never possible, and the implicit forms of love are the only way for them to love until their death. Even though for most people these forms of love never become direct, nevertheless these implicit loves can be love *for God*, and are under no circumstance valueless. For a few people – those who learn the lessons of affliction or joy – the implicit forms of love can grow so strong that they are subsumed and perfected, until they become direct forms of love for God. Even in its unperfected forms, implicit love of God can sometimes, Weil continued, reach a high degree of purity and power and even possess the virtue of sacraments. In any case, however, implicit forms of love for God must always precede direct love for God.

The first implicit love of God is love of our neighbour. In the parable of the sheep and the goats (Matthew 25.31–46) Jesus suggested that whoever gives to someone who is afflicted is in some sense giving to Christ himself. Within this statement, however, Weil perceived a paradox:

> Who but Christ himself can be Christ's benefactor? How can a man give meat to Christ, if he is not raised at least for a moment to the state spoken of by Saint Paul, when he no longer lives in himself but Christ lives in him?
>
> (WG 77)

As well as being present in the person who receives, as Jesus' parable suggests, Weil implied that Christ is in some sense present in the person who gives. What she meant by this difficult interpretation of Jesus' parable is that the spiritual worthiness of the person who gives has little to do with the value of the gift. In a service of holy communion, bread is passed from the priest to the believing communicant. But this sanctified bread is not simply being given by the priest: it is also mysteriously the gift of God. The worthiness of the priest is irrelevant, because the important thing is that it is God who gives the gift. Similarly, with an act of charity. Christ can make holy the gift of even a sinful person to someone in need. Thus, in addition to being an act of fellowship between donor and recipient, an act of charity also involves participating in the pure love of God.

Weil also believed that it is impossible to conceive of love in isolation from justice. That is to say, as well as having the qualities associated with love, an act of charity must also have within it the qualities associated with justice. When one person or group of people is in a position of power, Weil argued, their natural response is to use their position of strength to exploit the weaker party. If it is possible to do so, the strong often impose their will upon the weak. However, when confronted by a neighbour in need, Weil argued that in order to be an act of true charity, this natural relationship of inequality must somehow be overcome. Otherwise, even when giving to a needy neighbour, the stronger party will actually benefit more than the one who receives their gift. It is easy on a small scale to understand what Weil means when we think of the way that giving money to charity often makes us feel good about ourselves. It may seem as though we are giving something away, but in fact we are in some degree bolstering our need to feel generous. Weil put it most sharply when she wrote that 'Almsgiving when it is not supernatural is like a sort of purchase. It buys the sufferer' (WG 104). The result of this, she thought, is that 'Beyond a certain degree of inequality in the relations of men of unequal strength, the weaker passes into the state of matter and loses his personality' (WG 80). However, in contrast, justice means that there is between stronger and weaker parties a relationship of mutual consent: 'The supernatural virtue of justice consists of behaving exactly as though there were equality when one is the stronger in an unequal relationship' (WG 100).

Once love for our neighbour is seen in this light, it becomes clear that helping the afflicted person should be a completely instinctive act. Some Christians, Mother Teresa of Calcutta, for example, believe that when they help a person in need they do so for the Lord's sake. Weil, however, argued that a person who exercises implicit love of God in love for the neighbour: 'would not think of saying that he takes care of the afflicted for the Lord's sake; it would seem as absurd to him as it would be to say that he eats for the Lord's sake' (GWG 94).

An act of charity is not at all a conscious act of service to God, but a simple and natural response to a person in need.

That it is natural, however, is to take nothing away from the value of a true act of charity. When we give to our neighbour, Weil believed a miraculous event takes place. The person giving projects him or herself into the affliction of the other person. Imagine a mother whose child is in pain. Every pain the child feels is also in a real sense felt by his or her mother. The extent of the mother's love is so great that she projects herself into her child and actually experiences their affliction with them. Weil argued that one of the consequences of true affliction is that it reduces a person from being a human being to being a thing, an object. When a master commanded a slave, the slave was not treated as a person at all, but as an object to be used. Affliction, too, reduces a person to being an object, robbing them of their human dignity. To Weil, therefore, one of the miraculous consequences of love towards the afflicted is that it restores their humanity to them. By projecting oneself into a person who has become a mere object, one gives to them the gift of one's own humanity.

This exchange of generosity and gratitude, when it is conducted in a relationship of just equality, is immensely costly to the person who gives. By sharing in the affliction of another, by becoming personally afflicted, one's own humanity is diminished; in Jesus' words, one denies oneself. Weil also believed that love for one's neighbour, like other implicit loves of God, is not confined to Christians alone, but is felt and expressed by those who are not members of the Church. In Jesus' parable of the sheep and the goats (Matthew 25.31–46), those who expressed implicit love of God by caring for those in need had apparently done so without being conscious that they were loving Christ: 'When was it that we saw you hungry and gave you food . . . ?'

The second form of implicit love is love of the order of the world. This complements love towards our neighbour and, in common with it, requires an act of self-renunciation. One example of this love is the celebration of beauty. However,

Weil argued that love for beauty was sadly absent from the Christian tradition, though she acknowledged several exceptions to this rule, among them the poem of St Francis of Assisi celebrating the beauty of creation. Beauty, Weil believed, 'is necessity which, while remaining in conformity with its own law and with that alone, is obedient to the good' (GG 148). What she meant by this is that a beautiful thing has no objective except to be beautiful. In this quality it is unique; only beauty is not the means to something else. Such true beauty is not affected by the passage of time. Thus, our appreciation of beauty on earth is one of the few ways we can encounter here below something of the nature of eternity. However, according to Weil, even the finest works of art or science cannot compare with the natural beauty of the universe created by God:

> The only true beauty, the only beauty which is the real presence of God, is the beauty of the universe. Nothing which is less than the universe is beautiful.   (WG 130)

The third form of implicit love of God is the love of religious practices, by which Weil meant the love that people have for a particular religious tradition. Religion, however, Weil believed is no more valuable a form of implicit love of God than the two previous forms:

> God is present in religious practices, when they are pure, just as he is present in our neighbour and in the beauty of the world; in the same way and not any more.
> (WG 135)

Usually, the form of religion that we love depends on where we were born. A person born into a Hindu family will love God implicitly in Hindu religious practices, while a person born into a Roman Catholic family will love God in the religious practices of Catholicism. Though there are countless ways in which different religions worship God, Weil argued that the basic virtue within each of them remains the same: it lies in the recitation of the name of the Lord. Such worship nevertheless remains an implicit, not a direct form of love for God.

The beauty of religions, Weil believed, lies in the intention behind them, and not in their outward forms. Thus, the building in which worship takes place can be ugly, or the priest corrupt, or the singing out of tune – none of this matters. To illustrate what she meant, Weil suggested that when a mathematician illustrates a mathematical proof on a blackboard or a piece of paper, the straight lines she draws are often not exactly straight, nor the circles she draws exact circles. Nevertheless, the theory she is illustrating remains perfectly true in spite of her imperfect drawing. Similarly with religions, it is the purity of their content, not of their outward form that is important. The believer fixes her attention upon this purity, and it is in this looking that salvation is to be found.

To these three forms of implicit love of God – love of neighbour, love of the order of the world, and love of religious practices – Weil added pure friendship. Friendship differs from love for our neighbour in that it is directed towards a particular person known to us. Charity does not discriminate between people, but goes out both to those we know and to those we do not know. In friendship, on the other hand, we learn to love someone close to us. The key to this as an implicit form of the love of God is that friendship does not seek to conform the friend to our own needs. When the motive for loving a friend is that they fulfil our own needs, Weil argued, the conditions of friendship are not genuinely fulfilled. True friendship involves 'a supernatural harmony, a union of opposites' (WG 126). Achieving this can only happen when a kind of miracle of selflessness takes place:

> When a human being is attached to another by a bond
> of affection which contains any degree of necessity, it is

impossible that he should wish autonomy to be preserved both in himself and in the other. It is impossible by virtue of the mechanism of nature. It is however made possible by the miraculous intervention of the supernatural. This miracle is friendship. (WG 156)

Each of these implicit forms of love for God, according to Weil, takes place only where Christ is present, even when they take place outside the boundaries of the institutional Church among non-Christians. Where they do happen, a path is opened up for the coming of God. Weil concluded that the indirect or implicit loves of God are somehow perfected when direct love between an individual and God occurs. Far from becoming worthless after direct love has taken place, implicit forms of the love of God become a part of our direct love for God.

Our neighbour, our friends, religious ceremonies, and the beauty of the world do not fall to the level of unrealities after the soul has had direct contact with God. On the contrary, it is only then that these things become real. Previously they were half dreams. Previously there was no reality. (WG 166)

One obvious question raised by Weil's exploration of implicit love for God is 'What would this look like in practice?' The concrete shape of a society that expresses love for neighbour, love for the order of the world and love for religious practices led Weil into an exploration of human nature and the need for roots.

4

The need for roots

In more ways than one the demolition of the Berlin Wall in 1989 redrew the map of Europe. Germany reunited and nations that had for decades been part of multinational countries now resurfaced or surfaced for the first time as nation states. As well as geographical boundaries, the collapse of communism also prompted the redrawing of intellectual and political boundaries. For almost half a century, since the end of the Second World War, the states of North America and Europe had lived in an uneasy state of equipoise, in which the capitalist West and the communist East balanced each other out as two mighty military and ideological blocs. When the Wall came down, it seemed as if the triumph of capitalism was complete: one influential political thinker, Francis Fukuyama, went so far as to hail 1989 'the end of history', the point at which the tortuous political journey of humanity had reached its final form in the economic and political systems of the capitalist liberal democracies. Europe's economies and the discipline of economics that reflected on them were also changing, both before and after 1989. After mid-century flirtations with alternative economic theories (namely those associated with Karl Marx and with J. M. Keynes, both of which in different ways encouraged a high degree of state involvement in the economy), in the second half of the twentieth century most capitalist countries were returning to older predominantly laissez-faire models of economic management, in which the aim was to achieve a more or less self-regulating equilibrium between money and labour. Many of the heavy industries of the Industrial Revolution – coal mining, steel-making, ship-building etc. – were forced to close by rising competition from newly developed economies in Asia, while new jobs (eventually) emerged in the 'service sector'. Across Europe mills are being transformed into fashionable quayside apartment blocks; shopping malls and leisure centres are popping up where factories once stood; and in lucky mining towns, slag heaps have become all-weather ski slopes.

Much more could be said about social and cultural changes in Europe and in North America, for example changes arising from the larger number of women in work in the second half of the twentieth century. For our purposes, however, even this abbreviated summary suffices to make clear that many of the political themes to which Weil turned her attention seem oddly antique to readers at the beginning of the new millennium. Colonialism, Marxist economic and political analysis, workers' revolution, fascism, the experience of workers in heavy industry: all of these were live issues for Weil, but for most of her readers today they constitute a political agenda belonging to a rapidly fading era that it is now difficult to get worked up about.

Part of the delight to be found in reading Weil's social and political writings is, therefore, that in spite of the passage of time, they can still provoke thought, challenge settled views and illuminate previously unexplored corners of human sociality. At first glance, Weil's social and political writings don't seem to have much to do with her writings on religious or spiritual themes. Certainly, it is possible to read them simply from the viewpoint of political philosophy. But one does not have to be very long in Weil's company before easy distinctions between politics and religion begin to break down. Whether it be a connection between Weil's experience of work in the factory and her thinking about affliction, between her reflections on human rights and human personality and her writings on decreating the self, or between her critique of revolution and her suspicions of the Great Beast – those human societies that subordinate individuals to a collective goal – her writings resist compartmentalization. Indeed, readers of Weil break roughly into two groups: those who are only interested in a single aspect of her thought (her philosophy, her politics or her spirituality) and those who recognize her particular genius as lying in the rich cross-fertilization she achieved (or sought to achieve) between what most wish to view as discrete disciplines. In what follows, though the focus is on Weil's social and political thought, the connections between politics, philosophy and religion are never very far away.

Oppression and liberty

Wherever there was a choice to be made, Weil was on the side of the underdog. The writings of Karl Marx (1818–83) were an obvious initial resource for someone seeking to understand how the poor are oppressed. Weil believed that Marx had given 'a first-rate account of the mechanism of capitalist oppression' (OL 39). Marx's great discovery, for Weil, was that social oppression was not arbitrary or accidental, but happened as a direct result of the way in which modern societies worked:

> For Marx showed clearly that the true reason for the exploitation of the workers is not any desire on the part of the capitalists to enjoy and consume, but the need to expand the undertaking as rapidly as possible so as to make it more powerful than its rivals.   (OL 39)

Marx believed – rightly according to Weil – that ideas should lead to action and that philosophy should aim to change the world. But to change things, one must first understand how different groups in society depend on or exploit one another. It should not be assumed that the workings of society and the economy are wholly random. Rather,

> A methodological improvement in social organization presupposes a detailed study of the method of production,

in order to try to find out on the one hand what we may expect from it, in the immediate or distant future, from the point of view of output, and on the other hand what forms of social and cultural organization are compatible with it, and, finally, how it may itself be transformed.

(OL 44)

Such methodological study is now called the materialistic method, but there was a problem, Weil believed, with Marx's application of it:

> The materialistic method – that instrument which Marx bequeathed us – is an untried instrument; no Marxist has ever really used it, beginning with Marx himself. The only really valuable idea to be found in Marx's writings is also the only one that has been completely neglected. (OL 44)

Instead, what Marx had unwittingly achieved was to build a series of myths into a system without any real content.

One barrier to understanding Marx's thought and achievement was that Marxists took this flawed system and transformed it into an unchangeable doctrine. Weil, however, insisted that not even Marx was more precious than truth:

> To my mind, it is not events which make a revision of Marxism a necessity, it is Marx's doctrine, which, because of the gaps and inconsistencies it contains, is and always has been far inferior to the role people have wanted to make it play; which does not mean to say that either then or since anything better has been worked out. (OL 138)

The 'Red Virgin' also had something to say about another of the far Left's most deeply held aspirations – a revolution of the workers. 'The word "revolution",' she wrote, 'is a word for which you kill, for which you die, for which you send the labouring masses to their death, but which does not possess any content' (OL 53). Why, Weil questioned, should society get better because of a revolution? Marx asserted that societies pass through several recognizable stages, from rural to industrial, and through revolution to an idealized communist system. He believed, moreover, that these changes represented human progress, and that this progress could and should be guided by communist leaders. Weil, however, was suspicious of the possibility that revolution could effect human progress because 'The future is made of the same stuff as the present' (SNLG 148).

From her knowledge of the Soviet Union Weil could see that even if the working class did stage a revolution, the basic conditions of workers' lives were not thereby greatly altered. Even with 'regime change' the working classes of the Soviet Republics continued to labour in the factories or in the fields for long hours without much evidence of greater rewards. What difference did it make who owned the means of production if factory life continued to be oppressive? As long as workers felt like cogs in the factory machine, it did not matter whether it was a capitalist 'baron' who employed them, or the Soviet state.

Weil became increasingly sure that the answer to oppression of working people must lie beyond Marxist doctrine. By 1933 she concluded:

> I have decided to withdraw entirely from any kind of political activity except for theoretical work. That does not absolutely exclude possible participation in a great spontaneous movement of the masses (in the ranks, as a soldier), but I don't want any responsibility . . . because I am certain that all the blood that will be shed will be shed in vain.
>
> (Simone Pétrement, *Simone Weil: A Life*, p. 198)

The experience of work

One of the most important reasons, Weil thought, why left-wing thinkers had not understood the limitations of their theories was that none of them had experienced physical labour. This was her main reason for deciding to go 'undercover' to work as an un-skilled factory labourer, though she was also convinced that she needed to do this to model a way of breaking down the sharp division between manual worker and intellectual that, in her view, bedevilled much leftist political rhetoric. When, in 1934, Weil began work as a labourer, she anticipated being able to reflect on her experiences in order to sharpen up her theories. It immediately became apparent, however, that the physical and psychological effort required to operate the factory machinery was so intense that it would leave her neither time nor energy to think properly:

> ... the women ... are restricted to purely mechanical labour, in which nothing is required from them except speed. And when I say mechanical labour, don't imagine that it allows of day-dreaming, much less reflection or thought.   (SL 11)

Weil also found herself unable to keep up with the required rates of work:

> Yesterday I was on the same job the whole day (stamping press). I worked until 4 o'clock at the rate of 400 pieces an hour ... and I felt I was working hard. At 4 o'clock the foreman came round and said that if I didn't do 800 he would get rid of me.   (SL 17)

She attributed her inability to keep up to her unfamiliarity with physical work, her bodily awkwardness, her headaches and her habit of thinking too much. She concluded that to cope with factory life one must either be detached or 'fall to the vegetative level'. So unsuited was she to the work that she believed 'they would throw me out if I wasn't protected by influence' (SL 11).

Worse than the physical hardship, however, was the overall effect of factory life on Weil and on those around her. Socialist and communist art tended to idealize workers in picture and sculpture; in the years following the fall of the Berlin Wall one could still see, in former communist cities, colossal statues on roundabouts and in city squares, of men and women workers, tools of their trade in hand, striding confidently towards a socialist future. What Weil saw around her in the factory were men and women being stripped bare of their human dignity. Several factors contributed to this process of dehumanization. One was the way some foremen habitually humiliated the workers in their charge. Weil recorded one such incident in her journal:

> The machine's belt was adjusted before I worked on it, but incorrectly, it seems, for it rides over the edge. Mouquet [the foreman] orders it shut off . . . and says to Biol, 'The pulley has shifted, that's why the belt rides off.' Biol, eyeing the belt thoughtfully, starts a sentence: 'No . . .' and Mouquet interrupts him: 'What do you mean, No! I say Yes! . . .' Biol, without a word of reply, goes to find the guy in charge of repairs. As for me, fierce desire to slap Mouquet for his peremptory manner and his humiliatingly authoritarian tone of voice.   (FW 170)

But it was not merely a few obnoxious individuals that made factory life degrading. Weil believed there was something wrong at a much deeper level. Of profound significance was the 'mystery' of the machine. The manufacture of a finished product had been broken up into dozens of separate processes, each machine performing only one part in an overall process of production. To the workers, the way these different processes fitted together was a complete mystery. The effect of this was to make the human machine operators feel as though they themselves were part of the machinery. Without understanding the principles of production the workers experienced no sense of participation in the process. They had no pride in their work, and turned up each day purely and simply to earn enough money to feed themselves and their families. Weil viewed this way of life with a pity that is nonetheless shot through with a shaft of light. In a notebook entry she reflects:

The spirituality of work. Work makes us experience in the most exhausting manner the phenomenon of finality rebounding like a ball; to work in order to eat, to eat in order to work. If we regard one of the two as an end, or the one and the other taken separately, we are lost. Only the cycle contains the truth. A squirrel turning in its cage and the rotation of the celestial sphere – extreme misery and extreme grandeur. It is when a man sees himself as a squirrel turning round and round in a circular cage that, if he does not lie to himself, he is close to salvation . . . The great hardship in manual work is that we are compelled to expend our efforts for such long hours simply in order to exist. The slave is he to whom no good is proposed as the object of his labour except mere existence. (GG 179–80)

To work without any other goal than survival, to work simply in order to live, was, for Weil, not really living at all, but a kind of walking death. This was the situation of many of those around her; perhaps, in spite of many changes in the world of work (at least in most developed countries), we may say that it remains the condition of many still today. Weil could see, however, that honestly to recognize the condition under which one laboured was to bring oneself close to achieving a new relation to work, one in which an integration between life and work might be achieved.

After her year in the factory was over, Weil began to tease out her tangled thoughts about work. Several potential practical improvements to factory life were immediately apparent to her. In order to counterbalance the effects of the mass-production line, Weil had two main suggestions. First, she was convinced that labourers needed the ugliness of their lives to be complemented with beauty:

Workers need poetry more than bread. They need that their life should be a poem . . . Deprivation of this poetry explains all forms of demoralization. (GG 180–1)

Weil believed that employers had a responsibility to provide classes for their workers where there would be opportunity to study literature. Her studies of Homer's *Iliad* illustrate the kind of classes she had in mind. More realistically, perhaps, she believed that if workers could be taught to understand some of the basic principles of science, they might better understand the manufacturing process and feel more involved in it. Weil's second main suggestion was that if machines could be individualized, work might become more satisfying and production rates consequently rise.

Weil also reflected upon the nature of work, by which she always meant physical labour in the factory or in the field. Even before her first-hand factory experiences Weil had argued that it was essential that the gap between physical and intellectual labour be bridged:

> The only hope of socialism resides in those who have already brought about in themselves, as far as possible in the society of today, that union between manual and intellectual labour which characterizes the society we are aiming at. (OL 22)

Workers were not given the time or the education to think, while intellectuals lacked the experience of work. Weil envisaged a working people's culture in which work, science and art would complement one another as equal partners in the task of building society:

> Through work [man] produces his own natural existence. Through science he recreates the universe by means of symbols. Through art he recreates the alliance between his body and his soul. (GG 178)

From a Christian perspective, there is nothing unusual about understanding work positively as a sharing in God's creation. George Herbert, the English poet so admired by Weil, had written three centuries earlier:

> Who sweeps a room, as for thy laws,
> Makes that and the action fine.

But Weil did not believe that work was good because it was
a sharing in God's recreation of the world. On the contrary,
Weil's experience exposed a flaw in this Christian sentimen-
talization of work. Herbert had written of 'drudgery divine',
yet work as experienced on the factory floor was degrading
and filled the soul with disgust. This disgust, Weil argued, had
to do with the 'burdensomeness of time'. Time, which seems
to pass quickly when one is enjoying oneself, or when both
hands and mind are occupied, drags on interminably when
we are doing something we hate. It is 'effort without finality',
for 'Work is like a death if it is without an incentive' (GG 181).

Weil's powerful simile, in contrast with other Christian atti-
tudes to work, makes clear the physical and spiritual cost of work.
Work can exhaust body and soul and deprive them of the light
of eternity. At this point, it is worth recalling Weil's description
of affliction as 'an uprooting of life, a more or less attenuated
equivalent of death, made irresistibly present to the soul by
the attack or immediate apprehension of physical pain' (WG
77). Both affliction and work are likened to death, affecting
body and soul together. But these are not the only similarities
between them. Even though work, like affliction, is abhorrent,
when we submit to its necessity it can be a gateway to God:

> Manual labour. Time entering the body. Through work
> man turns himself into matter, as Christ does through
> the Eucharist. Work is like a death.
>
> We have to pass through death. We have to be killed –
> to endure the weight of the world. When the universe
> is weighing upon the back of a human creature, what is
> there to be surprised at if it hurts him? . . .
>
> To work – if we are worn out it means that we are
> becoming submissive to time as matter is. Thought
> is forced to pass from one instant to the next without

laying hold of the past or the future. That is what it
means to obey.   (GG 181)

In this way, Weil argues that the most important characteristic of work is not the way it enables a human person to participate in the *recreation* of the world, as Christian theology
had previously suggested, but the way it enables a person to
decreate herself. By submitting oneself to work, to the burden
of time and the reduction of one's humanity to bodily movement, the ego is dissolved and a vacant space opened to the
love of God. In a pregnant aphorism, Weil even parallels the
potential of work to transform human flesh to God's self-
giving as body and blood in the Eucharist:

> Catholic communion. God did not only make himself
> flesh for us once, every day he makes himself matter in
> order to give himself to man and to be consumed by
> him. Reciprocally, by fatigue, affliction and death, man
> is made matter and is consumed by God.   (GG 34)

To Weil, work is therefore one of the most atrocious experiences, but also potentially one of the most beautiful.

Weil's personal experience of work lends tremendous power
to her reflections. The practical suggestions she makes to
ameliorate these effects should be treated with the utmost respect. However, her reflections on work rest upon a troubling
contradiction. On the one hand, Weil recognizes the degrading effects of work and the way it disgusts the soul; factory
life is dehumanizing and everything must be done to improve
its conditions. On the other hand, she argues that work is to
be submitted to, as fatigue is a means of taking into one's body
the burden of time, of decreating the self – it is a gateway to
God. Workers, indeed, are peculiarly privileged, since the dehumanizing effect of work also removes any barrier between
God and the worker, stripping them of all that is superfluous.
Are Weil's social concerns in tension at this point with her

portrayal of work as a way to God? She solves this dilemma once more by means of the notion of contradiction:

> All true good carries with it conditions which are contradictory and as a consequence is impossible. He who keeps his attention really fixed on this impossibility and acts will do what is good. In the same way all truth contains a contradiction. Contradiction is the point of the pyramid. (GG 98–9)

To Weil, both the horror and the beauty of work are true, and their apparent contradiction is a sign of their truth. Weil believed everyone should work, and in spite of (or because of) her struggles with her own physical frailty at work, she was eventually to find a kind of tranquillity when hard at work in Gustave Thibon's fields. Work – and she meant by that always physical work – is a way of submitting to necessity that puts us in contact not only with our true humanity, but with God. This alone is enough to give pause for thought in societies where our contact with the earth and with the din of the production line are mediated entirely through supermarket and showroom:

> It is not difficult to define the place that spiritual labour should occupy in a well-ordered social life. It should be its spiritual core. (NR 298)

What makes a person sacred?

In 1943, while working for the Free French in London, Weil returned to social and political themes. In several essays she proceeded far beyond her interests in Marxism and work, towards an exploration of the fundamental needs of human beings. In the contemporary political debates of Western countries, one of the concepts most frequently resorted to is that of 'human rights'. In 1948, the countries of the United Nations agreed a 'Universal Declaration of Human Rights', a charter of civil and political rights essential to all individuals.

It included the rights to education, to equality before the law, freedom of religion and the right to life. The discourse of human rights has become, within Western politics and culture at least, a touchstone for much of what passes for conversation in the public square of good and evil, of right and wrong.

To Simone Weil, however, to make human rights the basis of culture is to commit a grave error:

> The notion of rights, which was launched into the world in 1789, has proved unable, because of its intrinsic inadequacy, to fulfil the role assigned to it.   (SE 10)

The first reason that the notion of human rights has failed, Weil argues, is because it is itself based upon a fundamental misconception of what it is about human beings that is sacred and inviolable. Proponents of human rights believe that the most valuable aspect of a human being is that part of them that is unique, their 'person', or their 'personality'. In her essay on 'Human Personality', however, Weil argues that: 'There is something sacred in every man, but it is not his person. Nor yet is it the human personality' (SE 9). Even our use of language demonstrates this point. We cannot, for example, say to someone 'You do not interest me' without offending against justice. But, Weil argues, it is not in the least offensive to say to someone 'Your person does not interest me': the *real* me, and the *real* you lie deeper than the outward trappings of 'person' and 'personality'.

Weil clarifies the subtle distinction she draws between person/personality and the sacred in each human being with an illustration. She imagines meeting a passer-by in the street. His appearance is distinctive but it is not this that is important, nor is it some hidden inner part of him, his distinctive 'personality'. If it is some hidden inner 'soul' that is sacred, what is to stop someone from poking out his eyes, since even blinded, he still has as much *personality* as he had before? In this way, she argues, the limitations of the concept of personality are laid bare.

It is impossible to define what is meant by respect for
human personality. It is not just that it cannot be defined
in words. That can be said of many perfectly clear ideas.
But this one cannot be conceived either . . .   (SE 9–10)

If it is not the person or personality in each human being that
is sacred, what is it? Weil answers that in her example what is
sacred in the passer-by 'is this man; no more and no less . . .
It is he. The whole of him. The arms, the eyes, the thoughts,
everything' (SE 9).

Though it is the whole of the man that is sacred, however,
he is not sacred in every respect. It is not because he happens
to have blue eyes, or because he has particularly wonderful
thoughts that he is sacred; nor is it some aspect of his person, for example that he is famous. His significance is the same
if he is a dustman or a duke. What is sacred in this man, Weil
concludes, is that if she puts out his eyes 'his soul would be
lacerated by the thought that harm was being done to him'
(SE 10). However, what would cause the soul to be hurt would
not merely be a sense of *personal* injury being done to the
body, but rather a sense that a universal injustice was being
done. In other words, Weil suggests,

When the infliction of evil provokes a cry of sorrowful
surprise from the depth of the soul, it is not a personal
thing . . . It is always, in the last of men as in Christ himself, an impersonal protest.   (SE 12)

Weil believed that deep within each person's heart there is a
germ of perfect good that has its origin in God. Such pure
good is only present in individuals and society in impercep-
tible quantities, but like the grain of mustard seed, or the hidden pearl of Jesus' parables, its effects are far-reaching. There
is nothing sacred in a person except this grain of perfect goodness, and perfection is by its very nature impersonal. Thus,
'far from its being his person, what is sacred in a human being

is the impersonal in him. Everything which is impersonal in man is sacred, and nothing else' (SE 13). In science it is truth that is sacred; in art it is beauty; in people and in society it is the germ of perfect good.

This complex argument may seem to make little difference to the success or failure of the notion of human rights. But Weil argues that when an appeal is made to the human rights of the individual, it is the rights of the person or personality that are being claimed, and not the deeper, more fundamental needs of the impersonal soul.

> The notion of rights is linked with the notion of sharing out, of exchange, of measured quantity. It has a commercial flavour, essentially evocative of legal claims and arguments. Rights are always asserted in a tone of contention; and when this tone is adopted, it must rely upon force in the background, or else it will be laughed at. (SE 18)

Rights are characterized by the desire to claim something from individuals or from society. In contrast, obligations are characterized by the imperative to give something. One result of this is that 'To place the notion of rights at the centre of social conflicts is to inhibit any possible impulse of charity on both sides' (SE 21). Weil is not arguing that rights are bad, nor is she suggesting that personality is bad or unimportant. Weil argues simply that obligations come first:

> The notion of obligations comes before that of rights, which is subordinate and relative to the former. A right is not effectual by itself, but only in relation to the obligation to which it corresponds, the effective exercise of a right springing not from the individual who possesses it, but from other men who consider themselves as being under a certain obligation towards him.   (NR 3)

While the germ of good, the source of the sacred in every human person, has a supernatural origin, the personality, and the rights associated with it, has its origins in the natural world. To this useful but secular sphere, Weil allocates rights, personality and democracy. In some limited sense, such notions have a role to play. Although the personal and the impersonal are in some respects opposed to one another, one can lead to the other, and thinking about rights can lead one towards the higher goods of truth, justice and compassion. However, as founding blocks of human life and society, these earthly notions on their own are very unreliable. Weil points out that we sometimes criticize people for pushing themselves (their *person*) forward; it is possible to speak of an *abuse* of democracy – Hitler was *elected* to office. Speaking of rights as though they are possessions implies that we can put them to both good and bad uses. In stark contrast, at all times and in all places, it is *good* to fulfil an obligation: 'Truth, beauty, justice, compassion are always and everywhere good' (SE 24).

For Weil, this curious argument about words (which suffers somewhat in translation from French to English) demonstrates that only supernatural good is effective in providing 'an armour for the afflicted'. There is, she points out: 'no guarantee for democracy, or for the protection of the person against the collectivity, without a disposition of public life relating it to the higher good which is impersonal and unrelated to any political form' (SE 34).

In her 'Draft for a Statement of Human Obligations' (SE 219–27), and in the first part of *The Need for Roots*, Weil spells out what it means to live as though the higher 'reality is the sole foundation of the good'. Even though this higher reality is beyond the reach of human faculties, men and women can choose to turn their attention towards this good and make it the real goal of their lives. Far from being an activity that leads to a neglect of obligations in this world, attention to the higher good 'is the only possible motive for universal respect towards human beings' (SE 220).

All people are different, and our natural instinct is therefore to respect some people more than others. However, argues

Weil, if what we respect in others is the *impersonal* link that every person has to the higher good then we learn to respect everyone equally, irrespective of creed, race or social status. Because pure good is inaccessible to human perception, expressing respect for the impersonal can only be done indirectly, by recognizing the obligation all people have to respect the needs of the soul and the body in this world. Needs and obligations are closely linked:

> The possibility of indirect expression of respect for the human being is the basis of obligation. Obligation is concerned with the needs in this world of the souls and bodies of human beings, whoever they may be. For each need there is a corresponding obligation; for each obligation a corresponding need. (SE 221–2)

The needs of the body are very clear: food, warmth, sleep, health, rest, exercise and fresh air. The needs of the soul are more difficult to enumerate and explain, and it is difficult to compile a complete list. There are, consequently, some differences between the list of the needs of the soul drawn up in her 'Draft for a Statement of Human Obligations' and that in *The Need for Roots*. For example, 'privacy' and 'social life' appear in the former, though not in the latter. Nevertheless, the principles remain the same. In her 'Draft for a Statement of Human Obligations' Weil lists the soul's needs in 'pairs of opposites which balance and complete one another' (SE 224). Examples of these are the needs of the soul for equality and hierarchy; for consented obedience and liberty; for truth and freedom of expression. For each pair of opposites, Weil offers a brief commentary. Concerning equality and hierarchy she writes:

> Equality is the public recognition, effectively expressed in institutions and manners, of the principle that an equal degree of attention is due to the needs of all human beings. Hierarchy is the scale of responsibilities. Since

attention is inclined to direct itself upwards and remain fixed, special provisions are necessary to ensure the effective comparability of equality and hierarchy.   (SE 224)

In *The Need for Roots*, Weil offers fuller explanations of the needs of the soul as examples of the kinds of investigations governments need to undertake if they are to avoid acting sporadically and at random. In subsequent sections Weil explores more deeply the experience of uprootedness. She also proposes examples of natural environments that need to be created for new roots to be grown:

To be rooted is perhaps the most important and least recognized need of the human soul. It is one of the hardest to define. A human being has roots by virtue of his real, active and natural participation in the life of a community which preserves in living shape certain particular treasures of the past and certain particular expectations of the future.   (NR 43)

In the period leading up to the Second World War, and more so following France's surrender, people had experienced uprootedness in town, countryside and in their nation. Weil argued that in order to set down roots, the soul would need new and healthy environments: people need to take root in a country; in a place where their language is spoken and in which there is a shared cultural and historical heritage; in a professional milieu; and in a local neighbourhood.

One example of such an environment is the nation. Weil recognized that 'there is no other way of defining the word nation than as a territorial aggregate whose various parts recognize the authority of the same State' (NR 95). But she also knew that there were limitations to this definition. One limitation was that, especially in times of war, people make the nation an absolute moral value. Others are hated purely because they do not belong to *my* nation. However, Weil argued, 'To posit one's country as an absolute value that cannot be defiled by evil is manifestly absurd' (NR 130). Nationalism does not mean having pride in one's country to the extent that it dissolves all other moral values. To love one's country means, rather, to have compassion for its needs; not to love it for its glory, but to love all within it that can be destroyed 'and is all the more precious on that account' (NR 170). To love one's country in this way illustrates what it means to have set down roots, and shows the damage done by being uprooted from this precious natural environment.

Weil understood that to express respect for human needs in a constitution, in laws, and in the life of a nation was a formidable task. 'Four obstacles', she wrote,

> separate us from a form of civilization likely to be worth something: our false conception of greatness; the degradation of the sentiment of justice; our idolization of money; and our lack of religious inspiration. (NR 216)

Plato's cave

In the essays she wrote in London in 1943, Weil put into the concrete form of ethical proposals the more abstract reflections of her earlier religious thought. Themes developed during her time in Marseilles, such as her concept of the good or of attention, are applied in these essays to the concrete problem of shaping society in post-war France. De Gaulle may have consigned these essays to his waste-paper basket, but they are among Weil's most enduring achievements. However, one idea that lies behind each of these essays needs to be brought into the open.

Weil's reflections on the sacred good latent within the individual, on obligations and on the needs of the soul, have their origin in her particular interpretation, first developed under

Alain's tutelage, of the philosophy of Plato. In order to glimpse something of Plato's role in Weil's thought (a role it is, however, certainly possible to *over*emphasize) it is helpful to recall a key allegory in Plato's philosophy, found in book VII of his *Republic*. In a defining moment in the dialogue, Plato has Socrates compare our life in the world to a number of men confined to living in a cave since childhood, their feet and necks bound by heavy chains in a way that obliges them to face the back wall of the cave. Behind them lies the cave's entrance, but because of their chains no one in the cave has ever been able to look round to see the sunlit entrance of the cave leading to the outside world. Within the cave, however, runs a low wall behind which is a huge fire. Between the fire and the wall walk a number of people. They themselves are hidden, but they carry on their shoulders all sorts of statues – of people and of animals – that cast moving shadows onto the wall that the men in chains are facing. In their ignorance of the outside world the men in chains believe that the shadows are real; they even give names to the moving shadows. This shadow life goes on until, by some freak of fate, one of the chained men becomes free. Some unknown force drags the liberated prisoner unwillingly towards the outside light. After the pain of refocusing his eyes in the dazzling brilliance of sunlight, he sees the real world, and finally learns that all the things he once thought real were actually poor shadows of reality. Returning to the cave the man tries to explain to his companions that their whole world is nothing but dim flickering shadows of reality. No one believes him, he is a laughing stock, and when he offers to set his companions free, they respond with incredulity, anger and fear.

Plato's story of the cave is a parable of the relationship of this earthly world to the higher reality of the supernatural world. As one would expect of a figure so central to Western philosophy throughout almost all of its history, interpretations of Plato – not least of what he intended in the allegory of the

cave – have been very varied. What concerns us here, however, is what Simone Weil understood Plato to mean. For Weil,
there were two basic points that one needed to grasp about
Plato. The first is that

> [h]e was not a man who invented a philosophical doc-
> trine. Unlike all other philosophers (without exception,
> I believe) he constantly reiterates that he has invented
> nothing and that he is simply pursuing a tradition, which
> he sometimes names and sometimes not.   (SNLG 91)

The second important point about Plato, for Weil, is that
the only writings by Plato that have survived are his popular
writings, intended for a general – not a specialist – audience.
This means that it is the responsibility of his readers to fathom
from hints in these popular writings what Plato thought.
Weil's conclusion (as we saw earlier in this book) was that
'Plato is an authentic mystic, and indeed the father of Western
mysticism' (SNLG 92). Weil thought that Plato is, in other
words (as her teacher Alain also believed), to be read as a poet
who carried his readers forward by means of image and
metaphor, to truth. Of course, poetry too can convey truth
about human life, about beauty, about love and about reality; indeed, there are some truths that are *better* conveyed poet-
ically than through philosophical (or theological) prose. For
Weil to describe Plato as a poet is, therefore, to honour him.

In the light of this, we need not read the allegory of the cave
as a prosaic account of the relation between two places that
exist in the same way – this world and the supernatural world.
We should, rather, read the allegory as a poem that tells us
something about ourselves and our situation. The cave is the
world; the chains are our impoverished imaginations. Plato's
parable teaches that our imaginations call us to make a painful
journey into the light of day, where truth, beauty, compassion
and the good are more real than anything we can imagine. These
ideals – truth, beauty, God – are not to be thought of as

objects in this world. They are separate, they are outside the cave where all human living occurs: in this sense, Weil can say, 'The wise have to return to the cave, and act there' (LP 221). It is the poets, not priests or philosophers or politicians, who are best able to struggle against incredulity and fear until they 'reach the stage where power is in the hands of those who refuse it, and not of those whose ambition is to possess it' (LP 221).

Weil's ideas about the ways in which individuals and societies grow roots have never been taken very seriously. Yet many components of Weil's essays on human personality, human obligations and the needs of the soul have value irrespective of whether or not we accept her 'mystical' description of reality. Her essays can be read as masterpieces of humanist values, admirable in their dogged idealism. Nevertheless, Weil wants to present her readers with a choice: do we agree or disagree with her that 'There is a reality outside the world, that is to say, outside space and time, outside man's mental universe, outside any sphere whatsoever accessible to human faculties . . . [and] just as the reality of this world is the sole foundation of facts, so that other reality is the sole foundation of the good' (SE 219)? Is she right? Does her reliance on Plato – and on the 'mystical' tradition she took him to instantiate and articulate – lead to a bifurcation of reality that ultimately distracts attention from this world by ever drawing the imagination towards another, ideal reality beyond? Is her thinking so drawn to the 'reality outside the world' that it is of no earthly use? These are some of the questions that are taken up in the final chapter, in which we may begin to see what may be made of Weil's legacy from the perspective of Christian theology.

5

Simone Weil: The last Cathar?

Ever since a priest in Marseilles deflected her enquiries by tell-ing her to direct her questions to someone better qualified to answer them, Simone Weil was haunted by the need to speak with a theologian. Weil was in conflict about the Church and its teachings and wanted a theologian not so much to resolve her conflict as to confirm her in it. A theologian, she thought, would tell her clearly and decisively that the religious convic-tions coagulating around her experience of Christ were unac-ceptable from the perspective of Catholic doctrine. In a letter to a priest explaining her hesitations about baptism, she con-veyed something of the pain involved in her decision. While, Weil wrote, she loved 'God, Christ and the Catholic faith as much as it is possible for so miserably inadequate a creature to love them', she was nonetheless restrained by her conscience from seeking baptism because 'I have not the slightest love for the Church in the strict sense of the word' (WG 19). While she loved the Church's hymns, its liturgy, its architecture, its sacraments, its saints and 'six or seven Catholics of genuine spirituality' she had met, the love of the Church required of a baptismal candidate was not (yet) her own calling. In her perverse and poignant spiritual logic, she had not yet reached the point at which 'I love God enough to deserve the grace of baptism' (WG 20).

As a Protestant, I am not the sort of theologian Weil had in mind as a conversation partner: she knew few Protestants and had read very little Protestant theology but was, regard-less, resolved to dismiss Protestants and their doctrines on the occasions she mentions them in her notebooks. Nonetheless, in what follows I want to begin to sketch an agenda for a theological commentary on several aspects of Weil's thought. The aim here is not to make a case against (or for) Weil's posthumous enrolment in the universal Church – as if, as a theologian, I were secretary of an elite club to which she had applied for membership. The question of whether Weil might in good conscience have entered the Church is, let us be clear, no longer an issue, and in the end, as the Psalmist says, 'Salvation belongeth unto the LORD' (3.8). Yet the question of whether Simone Weil had properly apprehended what Christians – Orthodox, Catholic and Protestant – believe about God, about creation, about Jesus Christ and God's relation to the world, remains one that deserves careful attention. If Christians are to benefit from the light Weil's writings may shed on the Christian gospel – as I believe they may – it is important that Weil's voice be heard not as a soliloquy spoken *to* theology but as part of a conversation in which Christian theology may respond as well as listen. To take us into some of the issues, I want to turn to Weil's attraction to the Cathars, that religious movement that flourished in what is now the Languedoc region of southern France, before it was brutally suppressed by the Albigensian crusades of the thirteenth century. As with our discussion of Plato in the last chapter, what matters here is less who the Cathars were, what they thought and what became of them, than how Weil appropriated their legacy in her own writings. Weil's attraction to the Cathars, their culture and their teachings, which developed during her two years in the Languedoc (see p. 14), has a good deal to say about her relationship to Christianity.

The perfect heresy

Strung out along a sun-baked ridge of the Montagne Noire in the Languedoc stand the four towers of the fortress of

Lastours, or Cabaret. Bounded on either side by rivers and accessible only by a steep and narrow path threading up from the valley below, Lastours is among the most romantic of the Cathar fortresses. Since the collapse of the Roman Empire, the Languedoc region had been a hotly disputed territory, regularly caught up in conflict, to which fortresses like Lastours bore witness. In the eleventh century, however, a series of judicious marital alliances brought peace to the region, allowing a distinctive culture to flourish based around the Occitanian language that gives the Languedoc – the language of 'Oc' – its name. This culture was characterized by an unusual degree of mutual tolerance between Catholic Christians and a heterodox religious movement known as Catharism. For a time, in the opening years of the thirteenth century, Lastours was a centre of that culture. Blessed by the presence of Etiennette de Pennautier, also known as Loba, and reputed to be the most beautiful maiden of her day, Lastours rejoiced in a succession of knightly lovers, poets and troubadours who beat a path to its doors in order to declare their ('platonic') love for the lovely *châtelaine*.

In 1198, the Catholic cardinals elected Innocent III as Pope. The first pope for two generations with both the initiative and the political backing to impose the Church's authority, Innocent decided to tackle the growing problem of the Cathar heresy flourishing throughout much of the Christian world, but especially in the tolerant environment of the Languedoc. At first he sent missionary preachers who tried to emulate the ascetic lifestyle of the itinerant Cathar preachers, but his initiative met with little success. In 1208, however, the atmosphere changed dramatically when a papal legate, Peter of Castelnau, was murdered, apparently on the orders of one of the Languedoc's leading noblemen. Innocent declared a crusade against the heretics and in the summer of 1209 the crusade took Béziers, the first of the Languedoc's cities in its path. In the name of Christ and of Pope Innocent, Christ's representative on earth, the crusaders slaughtered between 15,000 and 20,000 men, women and children of the city, Cathar and Catholic alike, in the course of a single day. Weeks later the crusaders, now under the command of Simon de Montfort, took the fortress of Bram, gouged out the eyes and sliced off the noses and tongues of its hundred defenders and, having left one man with an eye in order to lead the others, sent them on their way. In the late summer of 1209, therefore, it was a file of men very unlike any cheery procession of troubadours that picked its pitiful way to the gate of Lastours where, with what we may assume was a mixture of compassion and horror, the broken defenders of Bram were taken in. In 1211 Lastours surrendered to the crusaders without a fight. By the first quarter of the fourteenth century the Languedoc had been absorbed into the French kingdom and Catharism had ceased to exist.

The origins of Catharism are to this day difficult to pin down; their beliefs the more so, since much of what is known about Cathar theology comes from the predictably biased records of the Catholic Inquisition established to root out and prosecute their heresies in the wake of the Albigensian crusade. From the early centuries of the Christian era, Catholic orthodoxy had had to struggle with a series of heretical movements, each distinct yet with some common beliefs about God, Jesus Christ and the created order. In the first and second centuries of the Christian era the Gnostics taught that, at creation, souls had been trapped in matter and that Jesus Christ, the Primal Man, had come to bring a special knowledge – a 'gnosis' – that is able to liberate souls who accept and practise it in order to reunite their souls with God. One of their number, Marcion (who died around 160 CE), taught that matter was created by a Demiurge, to be equated with the God of the Hebrew Scriptures, with whom the God of Love revealed by Jesus Christ was locked in a battle for human redemption. In the third century CE, Manichaeism held that two worlds – the natural and the supernatural – were locked in a conflict, which their founder, a Persian named Manes, characterized in terms of a battle between light and dark, good and evil. A variant of the Manichaean heresy, known after its founder as Bogomilism, subsequently flared up in the tenth century, in what is now Bulgaria, and became the likely source of the Catharism of the Languedoc. Towards the end of the twelfth century, an anonymous but apparently well-informed writer from Lombardy – a stone's throw from the Languedoc – set out to describe the beliefs of the Cathars in *De heresi catharorum*. The Cathars, he wrote:

> believe and preach that there are two gods or lords without beginning or end, one good, the other wholly evil. And they say that each created angels: the good God good angels and the evil one evil ones, and that the good God is almighty in the heavenly home, and the evil one rules in all this worldly structure. (Malcolm Barber, *The Cathars*, p. 7)

The god of darkness, the god of this world, believed the Cathars, had a son named Lucifer, who inveigled himself into heaven, where he seized the souls of a number of angels and entrapped them in bodies that he placed in the world. The son of the good God, Jesus Christ, was sent to save those souls and restore them to heaven.

It is possible that the anonymous Lombard's report is not altogether accurate, and equally possible that the beliefs he describes represent the beliefs of only some Cathars. But there is no doubting that the gist of his report is true: the Cathars believed that this world is bad and that it should be the aim of every soul to shed its body and free itself from this world in order to find its way to heaven. Cathars didn't believe that Jesus Christ's incarnation, crucifixion and resurrection had literally taken place; that is, they did not believe that the son of the good God could possibly have taken upon himself the material flesh of a human body, since such flesh was evil. Jesus

Christ, they taught, bore the semblance of human flesh merely as a guise in which to preach his gospel of redemption. The Cathars accepted only one sacrament, the *consolamentum*, a once-in-a-lifetime ceremony that involved a candidate in saying the Lord's Prayer, culminating in the laying on of hands by any present who had themselves received the sacrament. The one who had received the *consolamentum* was termed a *perfectus* – one of the 'perfect' – and s/he subsequently abstained from meat, eggs and cheese, since all such foods came from animal bodies. The *perfecti* also undertook never to touch a member of the opposite sex. Some reports suggest that, very rarely, individuals who had received the *consolamentum* thereafter fasted until death in order to hasten the reunion of their soul with the good God. Surrounding the *perfecti* was a far wider community of sympathizers and seekers after truth, known as *credentes*: if one of them died before receiving the *consolamentum* their soul migrated into another body. Cathars did not believe in the resurrection of Jesus Christ, or the doctrine of the resurrection of the dead at the last judgment, since the resurrection of the body could only mean the eternal binding of good souls to evil matter. Though Cathar religion was to a certain extent organized – there were Cathar dioceses and bishops throughout the Languedoc – they despised the Catholic Church, regarding its representatives as servants of Lucifer.

The perfect heretic?

Like the Cathars, Weil treasured the Lord's Prayer. Like the Cathars she drew a fundamental distinction between the natural and the supernatural. Like the Cathar *perfecti* Weil was an ascetic: she eschewed rich food and led an asexual existence. Like the Cathars she sympathized with the views of Marcion, denied the canonicity of the Old Testament and thought that the God of love taught by Jesus was the antithesis of the vengeful and warlike 'god' of Jewish religion (SL 129). Like the Cathars Weil could see in the Church a modern reincarnation of the 'Great Beast' of imperial Rome. And like the Cathars, she taught the love of Jesus Christ and acknowledged the saving presence of God on the cross. Some critics have seen in her refusal of food towards the end of her life a curious echo of those few Cathar *perfecti*, typically women, who fasted in order to hasten death once they had received the *consolamentum*. Given such resemblances, is it meaningful to describe Simone Weil as the last Cathar?

The simple answer to that question is 'no'. The last recorded prosecution of an individual for Catharism took place in 1324; to call Weil a Cathar would plainly be an anachronism. Literally speaking, Weil herself understood that rebuilding the lost world of Cathar Occitania was as impossible as finding the lost city of Atlantis, since '[n]o one can feel any hope of reviving this land of Oc. Alas, it was too thoroughly killed' (SE 45). Yet Weil did not let that prevent her from believing that it was both possible and desirable to recover its essence, since '[t]he highest piety is a patriotic attachment to a dead country'. Far from putting her off, the fact that the religion of the Cathars had disappeared with the culture of thirteenth-century Languedoc, made its appeal all the stronger. Perhaps the attraction for Weil was that the lack of firm historical evidence about the lost civilization of Languedoc made it seem more purely spiritual:

> . . . we can only try to guess what this civilization was like – this civilization and all its works, which were destroyed by arms. The factual data are so few that we can hope only to discover its spirit and, therefore, although the poem [i.e. *The song of the Crusade against the Albigensians*] may give an idealized picture this does not make it a less useful guide; for it is the essential spirit of a civilization that its poets portray.   (SE 36)

What then was the 'essential spirit' of Catharism to which Weil was so attracted? Some of what Weil idealized in the dead culture of the Languedoc was, to be sure, concrete enough: she approved of the fact that it prized poetry so highly, and admired the apparent mutual tolerance between Catholic and Cathar. But what Weil chiefly saw in Catharism was the last living expression in Europe of that single train of mystical thought that she longed to dissolve her own thinking into. As she wrote in a glowing 'fan letter' to Déodat Roché, the early twentieth century's leading romanticist and myth-maker of Catharism:

> It is from this train of thought that Christianity issued; but only the Gnostics, Manichaeans, and Cathars seem to have kept really faithful to it. They alone really escaped the coarseness of mind and baseness of heart which were disseminated over vast territories by the Roman domination and which, still today, compose the atmosphere of Europe ... Catharism may be regarded as a Christian Pythagoreanism or Platonism; for in my eyes there is nothing above Plato. (SL 130–1)

The Greek vocation to articulate the purity of affliction was, as she put it, 'perfected by becoming the Christian vocation' (SE 46) but prevented from appearing – except in Catharism – by the twin imposition of Judaism and of Roman imperialism upon the gospel. For Weil, both Jewish religion and Roman imperialism worshipped force (see p. 33). The Cathars, by contrast, renounced violence, worshipped the God of love and perceived, as did Plato, that 'man's natural condition is darkness' (SE 53). For this reason Weil could write that among the aspects of the true and mystical 'train of thought' discernible in the spirit of Catharism was its orientation towards death, which is both the destiny and 'the annihilation of the limited being' (N Vol. 1 10).

Yet Weil was also able to espouse as truths beliefs that are far from easy to reconcile with what we know of Cathar theology. Because the Cathars believed that the material world was evil, they were bound to consider the incarnation of the son of God in human flesh a lie, since good and evil could under no circumstance be mixed together. And because they considered the incarnation of Jesus Christ in real human flesh a lie, the Cathars were bound to consider the Eucharist a fraud, since it signed the self-giving of Christ in the material elements of bread and wine. But Weil believed in both the incarnation and in the Eucharist. Indeed, though she had herself decided to live without sexual intimacy, she could even see in 'carnal love . . . a quest for the Incarnation', an attempt 'to love the beauty of the world in a human being' (FLN 84). And though, as we saw earlier, Weil could write in one note that resurrection proved nothing, in another she could write that:

> The resurrection is Christ's pardon to those who killed him, the evidence that in doing him the greatest possible harm they could do him no harm.   (FLN 69)

She could even go on to write, in a way that makes much clearer what she meant in her assertion that Hitler could rise 50 times without making him god, that:

> The joy of Easter is not the joy that comes after pain, like freedom after chains, repletion after hunger, or reunion after separation. It is the joy that soars above pain and perfects it . . . Pain and joy are in perfect equilibrium. Pain is the contrary of joy; but joy is not the contrary of pain.   (FLN 69)

In this insight Weil states in a distinctive way an insight common to mainstream Christian theology, which is that the cross and resurrection of Jesus Christ are two acts in a single drama. The Passion narratives of the Gospels narrate one act of God on behalf of humanity, following which Good Friday may never be sundered from Easter Day, nor Easter Day from Good Friday: 'no pain, no palm; no thorns, no throne; no gall, no glory; no cross, no crown' (William Penn). Weil could be similarly true to herself and richly theologically orthodox in relation to another Christian doctrine derided by the Cathars, the doctrine of the Trinity:

> The Father is creation of being, the Son is renunciation of being; this double pulsation is one single act which is Love or Spirit. When humility gives us a part in it, the Trinity is in us. (FLN 102)

What begins to emerge when we consider Weil's profound and richly orthodox reflections on these, the central doctrines of Christian theology – the incarnation of God in Christ, the integrity of cross and resurrection, and the Trinity – is that Weil's own claim to follow in a single train of thought running from classical Greek thought through Christianity to the Cathars, cannot be taken at face value. Her claim to see in the Cathars the essence of truth arises from her desire to side with the oppressed in a war in which the Catholic Church was the oppressor, and it arises from her conviction that the love and truth of God must be universally available, and not merely available to those baptized in the Catholic Church. Further than this, the details of what the Cathars really believed were something of an inconvenience, something to be overlooked. When it came to the Cathars, Simone Weil was more interested in seeing the wood than the trees.

This insight is telling, and brings us to the heart of the theological agenda that I, at least, would want to take up in conversation with Weil. The stumbling block standing in Weil's path is the scandal of the particular. That God should choose *this* people, the people of Israel, and no other in *this* moment of history, appalled her. That God should reveal Godself in Jesus Christ alone, without intimations of him before he was born or echoes of him after his death, seemed impossible to her. That God should choose *these* texts to witness to his life with Israel and with the Church and not others baffled her.

If Christ is one of a series of instances of God's self-disclosure in which humanity has had a share all the time, even if he is its supreme instance, what we have is not so much a decisive and unique event in Jesus Christ, but a supreme relativity. God was present for Weil in the ideal, rather than in the contingent: in *pure* joy and in *pure* affliction. She could believe that God loved the whole universe when he withdrew from creation in order to allow its being, but she could not grasp that this same God loved her, Simone Weil. She particularly admired in Catharism the teaching that one could love nothing that was not absolutely good and absolutely pure. For Weil, love for any this-worldly beauty, or love for a person, were implicit forms of the love of God; carnal love was a seeking after the incarnation of God. Christians, of course, believe God is absolutely good too, and also believe that what distinguishes Christians from others is that the love of God is their ultimate goal. The Gnostics, the Manichaeans and the Cathars were, to this extent, *Christian* heresies, parasitic upon a genuine Christian truth. But Christians also believe that God gives himself to us in *this* world and scandalously takes on the humiliation of sinful human flesh. Up to a point Weil believed this too; but she could not proceed from this to an understanding of the implications of God's love for us present in the contingencies of human life. Weil thought that love of God and of creation was to be learned from allowing oneself to become transparent to the love of God, to be dissolved by it. For Weil, tangled up in Plato's distinction between the natural and the supernatural, Jesus Christ showed the way from the natural to the supernatural. Plato's conceptualization of reality as divided between natural and supernatural realms, while it impacts upon Christian thought to a greater or lesser degree and from time to time, is finally transformed by a full understanding of the incarnation of Christ. A fully Christian understanding of incarnation maintains that in Christ, God overcomes the distinction between this world and the next world, the natural and supernatural, because in him, God enters the reality of the world. After the incarnation of Jesus Christ, what is Christian may *only* be had in what is worldly and the holy may *only* be met in the profane. What is more, the Christian Church makes clear that one of the ways God gives himself in the worldly is in the life of the Church. Christians believe the love of God is learned – at least in part – by participation in a community, the Church. In the Church, Christians believe, one learns the love of God not simply from direct encounter with God's perfection in prayer, but also in loving imperfect human beings and being loved by them, human beings who make mistakes and who grow through them in order to love each other as God first loved them. Without participation in such a community, without a sharing in the messiness of relationships not only with the Church's saints but also with its sinners, the way in which the narratives of God on *each* page of the Bible may become the word of God was lost on her. By regarding as scandalous the particularity of God's history with Israel; by placing the decisive and unique gift of Godself in Christ in a series of self-revelations; and in picking and choosing from the Bible only those parts that fitted in with the synthesis of truth she judged to be present in human history, Weil made herself into the ultimate arbiter of truth. She was a player in a truth-game in which she was also the umpire, able to change the rules to accommodate the hand she had been dealt. How are we to evaluate her legacy?

Evaluating Weil's legacy

Among Weil's greatest achievements is her attempt to achieve an interpenetration of thought and physical experience. By this means her debilitating headaches and physical frailty afforded profound insight into the meaning of affliction. Her experiences as a factory worker and as a refugee from the

Nazis motivated her to explore the value of work and the need for roots. Her experience led to ideas, and she struggled then to put her ideas back into practice. Weil argued forcefully that society has divorced physical labour from intellectual activity at its peril. Weil's life provides us with a model of how valuable can be the results when hand and brain work together. Weil is at her best in *The Need for Roots*, when her experience of physical labour and her insight into the realities of human needs combine to offer a vision for society based on obligations not rights. Her list of the needs of the soul and of the body, as compelling as they are original, have never yet been properly considered by politicians or legislators. The questions raised by Weil challenge the foundations of our society. Being critical of society is one thing, but Weil goes further: in *The Need for Roots* she offers alternative foundations that, if taken seriously, could be used as the basis of a society that might be more just and decent. In like manner, Weil was able to let her mind work on her raw mystical experiences in order to develop a rich account of the love of God.

Yet there is another side to the way Weil integrated thought and life. If we are prepared to believe that her thought may be somehow authenticated by the way it was integrated with her life, we must also be prepared to accept that her life may show up limitations in her thought. Weil insisted repeatedly that suffering must never be sought, while affliction must be embraced whenever it comes as a way of encountering God. In fairness, she also argued that joy was a gateway to God. The vital thing about both joy and affliction is that they must be accepted in their purest forms. Nevertheless, Weil undeniably put herself in the way of suffering. She laboured in factories when she was physically unsuited to the work, she sought danger in Spain, she became dispirited with the Free French because they would not give her a dangerous mission, and she went to the extraordinary extent of envying those who were paralysed. Even in more mundane matters, such as food and dress, she almost made a point of despising her bodily needs, which were always subordinated to her spiritual needs.

What questions are raised by the jarring tension between spirit and body in Weil's troubled life? Detachment, acceptance of the void, decreation, self-effacement: how are these themes in Weil's thought to be tallied with the incarnation of God in Christ? Here is paradox: 'This world is the closed door,' wrote Weil, '[i]t is a barrier. And at the same time it is the way through' (GG 145). Yet 'God crosses through the thickness of the world to come to us' (GG 90). The reality of this world, Weil says, is something we should detach ourselves from; yet it is in this world that God meets us. What is to be made of such thinking from the point of view of Christian theology, which teaches that: in Jesus Christ's incarnation God affirms the fundamental goodness of this world; in the cross of Jesus Christ God judges the world; and in raising Jesus Christ from death God transforms the world?

What then is true in Weil's thought? This question was the measure Weil herself set for her legacy: '[t]he eulogies of my intelligence', she wrote, 'are positively *intended* to evade the question: "Is what she says true?"' For those who read her today, however, more than ever truth is a difficult concept. The ersatz forms of tolerance on which much social intercourse and contemporary public debate trade mean that truth claims are often quickly denounced as attempts to force one's personal opinions on others. 'Truth' has become individual, personal: we speak as if 'this is true for me, though it may not be true for you'. Dogma, once the joyful teaching of truth, has become a dirty word, and to call someone 'dogmatic' is to accuse them of intolerance towards others. Simone Weil suspected dogma but asserted truth. She believed that divine truth ran through many religious and philosophical dogmas and she claimed to know truth from falsehood with Plato's help. She argued that the presence of the same religious beliefs in different traditions meant that they must be true. One such religious truth concerned the suffering of God. Thus it was that, though she knew Jesus was an historical figure and Prometheus 'merely' a literary character, she nonetheless drew parallels between the truths contained in stories of their suffering:

> 'My God, my God, why has thou forsaken me?' There we
> have the real proof that Christianity is something divine.
>
> (GG 87)

But why should suffering signpost the way to God? Why should *suffering* prove that something is divine? Weil believes this to be true because it has been taught by several religions in several eras. But the idea that God does not suffer and cannot suffer has also been widely taught. The Greeks took it to be a defining characteristic of divinity that a god cannot suffer. The philosophical term for the axiom that God cannot suffer is divine impassibility. Not only is this idea characteristic of Greek thought, it is present too in some Buddhist traditions as well as in classic Christian philosophical theology. On what grounds, other than her assertion that it is so, are we to know that suffering, and not impassibility is characteristic of God's relationship to the world? This is only one example, but there are others. Weil's repeated insistence that one should seek what is true in her writings begs the question about what truth is and how it may be discerned. Weil claims that we must seek truth, but is she right to assume that recognizing 'truth' is as straightforward for the rest of us as it was for her?

The questions raised here and in earlier chapters about aspects of Weil's thought are only a small proportion of the difficulties careful readers will find themselves struggling with in her writings. However, although 'truth' was the criterion Weil asked to be judged by, also important is her unerring ability to get to the heart of some of the key philosophical, theological and ethical issues of our time. Thus, though readers may not always agree with what she proposes, Weil belongs among those Christian thinkers who take us to the few most important questions about God and about life. One commentator has noted astutely that writing about Weil is like trying to advertise sunshine. Originality; the ability to strip away the dead wood of traditional theology and to bring fresh life to tired doctrines; courage in tackling social and political subjects from a Christian perspective – these are Weil's gifts. To dismiss them because Weil fails to fit comfortably into preconceived ideas of Christian theology will result in the impoverishment of us all.

Simone Weil was writing of the Christian gospel in a passage in her New York notebook when she remarked:

> If I light an electric torch at night out of doors I don't judge its power by looking at the bulb, but by seeing how many objects it lights up ... the value of a religious or, more generally, a spiritual way of life is appreciated by the amount of illumination thrown upon the things of this world. (FLN 147)

It may not have crossed Weil's mind to apply the analogy to her own writings, but we are at liberty to do so.

A guide to
further reading in English

Simone Weil published a relatively small proportion of what she wrote during her lifetime, and many of her writings take the form of notes, short essays and letters. As a consequence, they have tended to be published in collections of essays and papers, some of which in part overlap each other. In French, most of Weil's work was published after the war in *Collection Espoir*, a series edited by Albert Camus, a contemporary of Weil's and subsequent Nobel Laureate, who was a great admirer of Weil's work.

A helpful bibliography of writings by Weil and of books about her is included in:

Simone Weil: An Apprenticeship in Attention, Mario von der Ruhr, Continuum, London and New York, 2006, pp. 158–64.

Books, notebooks and essays by Simone Weil

The following is a list of texts by Weil referred to in this book. The abbreviations used to refer to them are given on p. x.

First and Last Notebooks, tr. and ed. Richard Rees, Oxford University Press, London, 1970: contains the notebooks from roughly 1933 to 1939, the notebooks written in New York in 1942 and in London in 1943.
Formative Writings 1929–1941, ed. D. Tuck et al., Routledge, London, 1987.
Gateway to God, eds D. Raper, M. Muggeridge and V. Sproxton, Collins/Fontana, Glasgow, 1974: a collection of extracts and essays; it includes three essays 'On the Love of God'.
Gravity and Grace, ed. and intr. Gustave Thibon, tr. Emma Craufurd and Mario von der Ruhr, Routledge Classics,

London and New York, 2002: a collection of extracts from Weil's *Notebooks*, this is a reasonable way to get a feel of the notebooks as a whole, although the selection and presentation bear the strong imprint of its editor (see p. 22).

Intimations of Christianity among the Ancient Greeks, Ark Paperbacks (Routledge), London, 1987: a selection of Weil's writings on ancient Greek tragedy and philosophy, including her essays on Antigone, on Prometheus and on God in Plato.

Lectures in Philosophy, tr. Hugh Price, Cambridge University Press, Cambridge, 1978: these are the transcribed notes of Weil's lectures by one of her pupils at the Lycée at Roanne. They are not a verbatim record of those lectures, but do succeed in giving a sense of the content and form of Weil's teaching.

The Need for Roots, tr. Arthur Willis; preface T. S. Eliot, Routledge Classics, London and New York, 2002.

The Notebooks of Simone Weil, tr. Arthur Willis, 2 vols., Routledge & Kegan Paul, London, 1956 [republished as a single volume, Routledge, 2004]: confusingly, these appear in three volumes in French but two volumes (or one combined volume) in English. Willis' translation is of the notebooks written between 1940 and 1942.

On Science, Necessity, and the Love of God, coll., tr. and ed. Richard Rees, Oxford University Press, London, 1968: contains Weil's fascinating essays on science, and the full text, extracted from her notebooks, of the important essay on 'God in Plato', a shorter version of which appears in *Intimations of Christianity among the Ancient Greeks*.

Oppression and Liberty, tr. A. Wills and J. Petrie, Ark Paperbacks (Routledge), London, 1988.

Selected Essays, sel. and tr. Richard Rees, Oxford University Press, London, 1962: includes the essay 'On Human Personality' and two essays on the Cathars.

Seventy Letters, tr. and ed. Richard Rees, Oxford University Press, Oxford, 1965.

Waiting on God, tr. Emma Craufurd, Fount Paperbacks (Collins), London, 1977: essays and letters, including 'Spiritual Biography' and the texts on 'Love of God and Affliction' and 'Forms of the Implicit Love of God'.

Anthologies

An obvious next step for an interested reader of this book may be to read an anthology of Weil's own writings. One such is:

Simone Weil: An Anthology, Simone Weil, Penguin Classics, London, 2005.

Books about Simone Weil

The following essays and books are among those I have found particularly helpful in preparing this book.

For Chapter 1: Simone Weil's life

Simone Weil, Francine du Plessix Gray, Weidenfeld and Nicolson, London, 2001: relatively short and very readable.

Simone Weil: A Life, Simone Pétrement, tr. Raymond Rosenthal, Mowbray, London and Oxford, 1976: this biography, by one of Weil's closest friends who was a fine scholar in her own right, is the leading biographical resource and manages successfully to marry affection for its subject with acute insight and evaluation.

Simone Weil: Utopian Pessimist, David McLellan, Papermac (Macmillan), London, 1989: McLellan, a political scientist, has a particularly good feel for Weil's political context and her engagement with it.

For Chapter 2: Weil's understanding of God

Arguments and Doctrines: A Reader of Jewish Thinking in the Aftermath of the Holocaust, sel. Arthur A. Cohen, Harper and Row, New York, 1970: see especially 'Simone Weil, prophet out of Israel' by Leslie A. Fielder and 'Contra, Simone Weil' by Hans Meyerhoff, pp. 50–85: both are provocative essays on Weil's anti-Judaism.

'The necessary non-existence of God', Rowan Williams, pp. 52–76 in *Simone Weil's Philosophy of Culture*, ed. Richard Bell, Cambridge University Press, Cambridge, 1993.

'Simone Weil against the Bible', Emmanuel Levinas, pp. 133–41 in *Difficult Freedom: Essays on Judaism*, E. Levinas, Johns Hopkins University Press, Baltimore, 1990.

For Chapter 3: Loving God in a world full of pain

'Simone Weil and Antigone: innocence and affliction', Anne Loades, pp. 277–94 in *Simone Weil's Philosophy of Culture*, ed. Richard Bell, Cambridge University Press, Cambridge, 1993.

For Chapter 4: The need for roots

The Christian Platonism of Simone Weil, eds E. Jane Doering and Eric O. Springsted, University of Notre Dame Press, Notre Dame, Indiana, 2004: a collection of essays dealing with various aspects of the relationship of Simone Weil's thought to that of Plato and of subsequent Platonic and neo-Platonic writers.

Simone Weil and the Politics of Self-Denial, Athanasios Moulakis, University of Missouri Press, Columbia and London, 1998: a sensitive and comprehensive study of Weil's political thought.

For Chapter 5: Simone Weil: The last Cathar?

The Cathars: Dualist Heretics in Languedoc in the High Middle Ages, Malcolm Barber, Longman, London, 2000: while there are several very good histories of the Albigensian crusade, few take as much trouble as Barber to get to the heart of what the Cathars believed and practised. Chapter 7 (pages 203–25) looks at 'Cathars after Catharism' and singles out Weil for attention.

The Perfect Heresy: The Life and Death of the Cathars, Stephen O'Shea, Profile Books, London, 2001: a lively popular history of the Cathars.

Index

Index